WAR AGAINST THE POOR

WAR AGAINST THE POOR

Low-Intensity Conflict and Christian Faith

Jack Nelson-Pallmeyer

ORBIS BOOKS

Maryknoll, New York 10545

The Catholic Foreign Mission Society of America (Maryknoll) recruits and trains people for overseas missionary service. Through Orbis Books, Maryknoll aims to foster the international dialogue that is essential to mission. The books published, however, reflect the opinions of their authors and are not meant to represent the official position of the society.

© 1989 by Jack Nelson-Pallmeyer
Published by Orbis Books, Maryknoll, NY 10545
All rights reserved
Manufactured in the United States of America

Manuscript editor: Lisa McGaw

Library of Congress Cataloging-in-Publication Data

Nelson-Pallmeyer, Jack.
    War against the poor: low-intensity conflict and Christian faith
/ Jack Nelson-Pallmeyer.
        p.   cm.
    Bibliography: p.
    Includes index.
    ISBN 0-88344-589-1
    1. Central America—Relations—United States.   2. United States-
Relations—Central America.   3. Low-intensity conflicts (Military
science—Central America—History—20th century.   4. Central
America—Politics and government—1979-   5. Church work with the
poor—Central America—History—20th century.   6. United States
—Military policy.   I. Title.
F1436.8.U6N45   1989
303.4'82728073—dc19   88-38165
                                                                  CIP

To my wife, Sara,
and
to our daughter, Hannah,
who was seven months old when I completed this book. I
am grateful to them both for their laughter and their love
and for teaching me that our family's future is intimately
tied to the well-being of the whole human family.

Contents

Introduction

As the leading "have" power, we may expect to have to fight to protect our national valuables against envious "have nots."

General Maxwell D. Taylor, U.S. Army

Our country has been converted into a proving ground for experimental political, military, economic and ideological projects developed in the White House and the Pentagon. Your government has become the center of domination and subjugation of poor peoples of the world such as ours: peoples with an unsatisfied hunger for justice, a deep thrist for a better and more humane future, and an unquenchable yearning for life. In each heart lies the certain hope, growing like a baby giant, of building peace with justice.

Herbert Ernesto Anaya, President,
Non-Governmental Human Rights Commission of El Salvador

I can understand how the [Nicaraguan] revolution cannot be very pleasing to the landholders since it took away the land they had piled up. Just as it can't be very pleasant for the gringos, since the revolution messed up their fat profiteering . . . .
. . . Spanish greed, English greed, American greed, one after another — always oligarchical greed. It's about time that the rivers of Latin America, the peoples of Latin America, be freed of these greeds of Latin America. For too long the powerful have sucked the blood out of the "open veins" of our Americas!

Pedro Casaldáliga, Bishop from Brazil

In the late 1970s and early 1980s Central America suddenly became the most important place on earth for U.S. policymakers. The Nicaraguan people's overthrow of a U.S.-backed dictatorship in 1979 and the existence of popularly based movements for social change throughout the region had caused great concern in Washington. "The national security of all the Americas is at stake in Central America," President Reagan had stated. "If we cannot defend ourselves there, we cannot expect to prevail elsewhere. Our credibility would collapse, our alliances would crumble and the safety of our homeland would be put in jeopardy."

El Salvador, and by extension the whole region, had been selected as "an ideal testing ground" for modern low-intensity conflict. The term itself is unknown to most U.S. citizens yet low-intensity conflict is the key strategy by which the United States seeks to project its power in the third world in order to protect perceived vital interests.

I have been living in, or a frequent visitor to, the Central American region since 1982. This book is in many ways a description of my own journey to understand the comprehensive nature and dangerous consequences of low-intensity conflict. Living and working in Central America, I witnessed a level of human suffering that would defy the imaginations of most U.S. citizens. The suffering endured by the people was often times not merely an unfortunate consequence of misguided U.S. policies but was in fact the actual goal of those policies.

In Central America I was confronted with a series of baffling questions:

● Why would the United States publicly condemn terrorism while at the same time create, fund and direct the contras in Nicaragua, whose principal tactic was terrorism against civilians?

● How could a popular, nationalistic revolution in the impoverished country of Nicaragua, a country with 3 million people, or in neighboring El Salvador constitute a threat to the security of the United States?

● Why did the United States work to undermine regional diplomatic initiatives such as the Contadora and Arias peace plans, which would have achieved goals publicly stated by the Reagan administration, such as no foreign military bases in the region?

● Why did major segments of the mainstream U.S. media allow U.S. government officials and agencies to determine the parameters of debate about the crisis in Central America? If the United States had a free press, then why were the U.S. people indifferent to or ignorant of the terrible human costs of U.S. foreign policy?

● If the United States were firmly committed to democracy, then why was Central American policy carried out against the wishes of the U.S. people and through clandestine and often illegal channels? Why did the United States label Nicaragua's elections "a sham" when they received widespread support within the international community? In what ways did U.S.-supported elections in El Salvador and elsewhere in Central America serve undemocratic purposes?

● Why was liberation theology, which seeks to awaken the dignity and hope of the poor, considered subversive and dangerous by low-intensity-conflict planners while religious philosophies that tolerated earthly misery and promised heavenly rewards received broad support?

The weight of human suffering in Central America led me to explore the theoretical and practical world of low-intensity conflict. The primary focus of this book is on U.S. low-intensity-conflict strategy in Central America because of my personal ties and experiences in the region. However, low-intensity conflict is a globalwide strategy played out in distinct ways in places like Angola, Afghanistan, and the Philippines. I hope that a detailed examination of Central America will shed light on U.S. policies elsewhere.

War against the Poor examines the stated and unstated assumptions of low-intensity-conflict strategy. The statements and position papers of U.S. policymakers when examined in light of my own experience and through the eyes of the poor have led me to disturbing, even frightening conclusions. I have come to believe that low-intensity conflict is for the United States a global strategy of warfare waged against the poor. Neatly packaged for public consumption, low-intensity conflict is like a deadly bomb wrapped with beautiful paper. It couples the use of explicit terror with rhetoric about "freedom," "democracy," and "national interest." When the wrapping paper is removed one sees how the unbearable suffering of the vast majority of people in Central America is the fruit of a calculated policy in defense of U.S. privilege.

The victims of low-intensity conflict are not limited to the poor. Also at stake is the future of our own democracy and the integrity of our faith. Low-intensity conflict is so broad in scope, so cynical in outlook, so damaging in practice that it presents Christians and churches in the United States with a situation similar to that faced by the Confessing churches in Nazi Germany. In short, low-intensity conflict presents us with a confessional situation that demands acknowledgment of our participation in a sinful situation, repentance, and creative action.

In chapter 1, "Redefining the Enemy," I describe the present global economic order as one in need of fundamental restructuring, and how the United States through low-intensity conflict seeks to block or control any such changes. The basic worldview that serves as the ideological basis for low-intensity conflict will be examined. This worldview regards changes in the present world order as communist-inspired threats against U.S. national security interests. The poor whose hopes for a dignified life or even survival depend on such changes are considered enemies.

Chapter 2, "The 'Crimes' of the Poor," will look more closely at the philosophy and actual reforms of the Nicaraguan revolution and the aspirations of the Salvadoran people. Nicaragua's efforts to address the needs of its poor majority by reordering political and economic life will be examined in order to explain why these changes are considered dangerous to U.S. interests. Lessons will also be drawn from the courageous example of the Salvadoran people as they work to challenge the old order and replace it with a system more responsive to human needs.

Chapter 3, "Low-Intensity Conflict: The Strategy," will examine the economic, psychological, diplomatic, and military components of low-intensity warfare, with specific examples drawn from U.S. policy in Central America. I shall analyze how low-intensity conflict is a comprehensive, totalitarianlike project through which the United States seeks to manage social change in the third world in order to protect perceived vital interests.

Chapter 4, "Distorted Democracy," will discuss how low-intensity conflict undermines democratic institutions at home and abroad. Democratic freedoms are, or soon could be, trampled on by the misuse of elections, disinformation campaigns, the concentration of economic power, and the abuse of presidential powers cloaked in the secrecy of covert operations.

Finally, in chapter 5, "Faith and Empire," I shall examine scriptural challenges to people of power by a God who works for the liberation of the oppressed within history. Low-intensity conflict, which defines the poor as enemy, is clearly in conflict with a biblical God who takes sides with the poor. Our challenge as Christians who are also citizens of an empire is to find hope and guidance in biblical calls to repentance and conversion that inevitably confront people whose historical ties are linked to dominant powers that come under the judgment of God. I shall explore what it might mean to live as a confessing people in the context of the radical sin of low-intensity conflict and how we can faithfully respond to the present historical moment in which our participation in the structures of oppression call us to be prophetic witnesses and living signs of hope.

WAR AGAINST THE POOR

1

Redefining the Enemy

Unfulfilled expectations and economic mismanagement have turned much of the developing world into a "hothouse of conflict," capable of spilling over and engulfing the industrial West. ... [T]he security of the United States requires a restructuring of our warmaking capabilities, placing new emphasis on the ability to fight a succession of limited wars, and to project power into the Third World.

Neil C. Livingstone,
Pentagon Consultant on Low-Intensity Conflict[1]

It is the lack of basic needs that most violates human rights. ... As hunger intensifies and housing deteriorates the people make organized demands and these demands are met with repression. ... The U.S. embassy is in agreement with our destruction. We are a thorn to be eliminated. ... Whatever germ of inequality is planted also is planted the seed of social injustice and the determination to transform the society. With our final breath we will continue our work. This isn't heroism. It is simply doing what we have to do.

Herbert Ernesto Anaya, President,
Non-Governmental Human Rights Commission of El Salvador

INTRODUCTION

Low-intensity conflict is an evolving strategy of counterrevolutionary warfare. It is the nuts-and-bolts means by which the United States is fighting a series of "limited wars" and projecting "power into the Third World." A counterrevolutionary superpower in a world of massive structural inequalities, the United States is actively engaged in a global war against the poor. "As the leading 'have' power," General Maxwell Taylor predicted in the aftermath of the Vietnam War, "we may expect to have to fight to protect our national valuables against envious 'have nots.' "[2] The defense of U.S. "national interests" or our "national valuables" necessarily conflicts with the needs of the poor whose hope for a dignified future, including freedom from misery, can be realized only in a world of greater social justice.

Low-intensity conflict is the latest chapter in a longer history of U.S. counterinsurgency warfare. It is not a rigid plan but an evolving project of interventionism that seeks to respond effectively to present and future challenges to U.S. power and control, particularly in the third world.[3]

Low-intensity conflict draws heavily from the successes and failures of previous U.S. counterinsurgency efforts. Covert operations that ousted the democratically elected reformist government of Jacobo Arbenz Guzmán in Guatemala in 1954 and the socialist government of Salvador Allende in Chile in 1973 have been thoroughly studied. More important, the failures of the U.S. war in Vietnam have been relived thousands of times in search of clues to more appropriate and successful forms of intervention.

Low-intensity conflict is in many ways a creative response to the limited usefulness of traditional U.S. military power and capabilities in third-world situations and to the apparent war weariness of the U.S. people. Its overall strategy is crafted to overcome the "Vietnam Syndrome," which from the point of view of U. S. economic and military elites is the lamentable reluctance of its citizens in the post-Vietnam era to support the defense of "vital" interests overseas through the projection of U.S. power, including deployment of U.S. troops.

Present-day low-intensity-conflict theory and practice draws heavily from previous "nation-building" efforts such as the Kennedy administration's Alliance for Progress. The alliance was developed in the 1960s in response to the ouster of a U.S.-backed dictatorship in Cuba and the coming to power of Fidel Castro. In an effort to manage or prevent social change within poor countries, low-intensity conflict and the alliance that preceded it integrate increased economic assistance, cosmetic internal reforms, and the training and management of repressive police and military forces within exploited countries.[4]

What separates low-intensity conflict from previous counterinsurgency efforts are its comprehensive nature and its broad-based support within military and non-military governmental circles. The development and implementation of low-intensity-conflict capabilities involves an unprecedented degree of coordination among the White House, the Joint Chiefs of Staff (and each of the military branches), the National Security Council, the Central Intelligence Agency (CIA), the State Department, the Agency for International Development, conservative private aid groups, and a shady semiprivate network of drug-runners, arms merchants, and assassins.

The elevation of low-intensity conflict to a higher status within defense planning reflects a reassessment of threats to U.S. security and a redefinition of "our enemies." It is now generally accepted by U.S. policy makers that the third world is the strategic center of international conflict and that low-intensity warfare is the most appropriate means by which the United States can defend its perceived interests.

The reassessment of security threats to the United States has led to a shift of financial and human resources to the development or expansion of Special Operations Forces (SOF) capable of intervening anywhere in the third world. Funding for SOF increased from $441 million in fiscal year (FY) 1981 to $1.7 billion in FY 1987 with an additional $8 billion projected for the years 1989–92.[5]

Casper Weinberger, secretary of defense throughout much of the Reagan presidency, told Congress in his 1985 annual report that expansion of Special Operations Forces are "one of this Administration's highest priorities."[6] "The particular skills and supporting capabilities which the military offers to the prosecution of low-intensity conflict," Weinberger stated elsewhere, "are chiefly to be found in our Special Operations Forces."[7]

THE DEFENSE OF EMPIRE

The acceptability of empire is the guiding principle that shapes U.S. foreign policy. The United States is battling to safeguard its power and privilege against millions of exploited people whose hope depends on a fundamental restructuring of the domestic and international orders that hold them in bondage. Whatever moral ambivalence might accompany this conflict between empire and the well-being of the poor is smothered under a landslide of rhetoric about "fighting communism" and promoting "freedom and democracy," or it is quickly passed over as a superpower's unavoidable dilemma.

We rarely apply the word "empire" to ourselves. "Empire" is a derogatory term used to describe our adversary and not a problem or a concept that might lead us to national self-reflection and repentance. The geopolitical reality is carefully framed in terms of a *benevolent superpower* (the United States) up against an *evil empire* (the Soviet Union). Our right to be an empire has been so thoroughly internalized that it has become a deep part of our national psyche without entering our vocabulary. The problems this raises for people of faith will be discussed later (chap. 5, below). What concerns me here is that low-intensity conflict is designed not only to defend the U.S. empire against rising challenges from the poor but also to conceal from U.S. citizens the unpleasant consequences of empire.

U.S. policymakers often speak honestly to themselves while consciously deceiving the U.S. people, whose sensibilities and basic decency they fear. "U. S. rhetoric is often noble and inspiring," writes Noam Chomsky, "while operative policy in the real world follows its own quite different course, readily discernible in the actual history." Chomsky notes that behind the "rhetorical flourishes of political leaders" is a real story of exploitation and terror that is "often outlined frankly in internal documents," but which must be concealed "from the domestic population . . . who would be unlikely to tolerate the truth with equanimity."[8]

Contrary to the popular view that U.S. citizens are the most and perhaps only objective people in the world, we may be the most effectively socialized. We have grown up on a steady diet of stories depicting the horrors of communism (some of them true) and our defense of freedom (most of them not true). I witnessed many hundreds of U.S. citizens arrive in Central America with a basic confidence in their government's policy. The vast majority left agonizing over the contradictions between the stated goals and means of official policy versus their experienced reality of U.S.-backed exploitation and repression throughout the region.

No amount of rhetoric can hide from a careful observer that in Central America, Eastern Europe, and elsewhere there is a fundamental and irreconcilable conflict between empire and social justice. Countries that live on the edges of either the Soviet or the U.S. empire experience similar, exploitative relationships.

The U.S. empire is motivated by its commitment to what Noam Chomsky calls a "Fifth Freedom," which is "the freedom to rob and exploit." "A careful look at history and the internal record of planning," Chomsky writes, "reveals a guiding geopolitical conception: preservation of the Fifth Freedom, by whatever means are feasible."[9]

Low-intensity conflict is descriptive of both the kinds of foreign-policy challenges the United States is likely to face and the U.S. response to those challenges. It is the foreign-policy strategy assigned the task of defending the empire by projecting power and influence throughout the third world where conflicts are real but where nuclear or conventional military responses are considered inappropriate. "The high priority we have assigned to SOF revitalization," Defense Secretary Weinberger stated in 1984, "reflects our recognition that low-level conflict—for which SOF are uniquely suited—will pose the threat we are most likely to encounter throughout the end of this century."[10]

Special Operations Forces are part of a multi-billion-dollar program to create, train, and equip new counter or proinsurgency forces capable of operating in every region of the third world. SOF carried out the attempted rescue of U.S. hostages in Iran in 1980, spearheaded the invasion of Grenada in 1983, and in violation of international law orchestrated the 1983 attack on the Nicaraguan port of Corinto. Stephen Goose offers the following summary of Special Operations Forces:

> SOF are the U.S. military's elite, highly trained commando units. They are sometimes called America's "secret soldiers," and include hush-hush units such as the Delta Force that the Pentagon will not even acknowledge exist. . . . SOF include the U.S. Army Special Forces (the "Green Berets"), the Rangers, the 160th Army Aviation Battalion, psychological operations and civil affairs units, the Navy's sea-air-land

(SEAL) commando forces, the Air Force Special Operations Wing and special-operations-capable Marine amphibious units (MAUs).

Special Operations Forces are America's experts in guerrilla and antiguerrilla warfare, in sabotage, and in counterterrorism operations. SOF . . . do "dirty jobs" — they are the forces that are usually ordered to carry out clandestine operations in foreign countries in peacetime. SOF learn to fight in any terrain, in any location in the world.[11]

Low-intensity conflict is as much a war of images, ideas, and deception as it is a war of bullets and bombs. Special Operations Forces include experts in psychological operations and civil affairs. The ability to create images that obscure reality is a powerful weapon to be directed against our own and other peoples.

Many U.S. policymakers recognize that real objectives must be concealed under an avalanche of positive rhetoric. They are concerned about the "Vietnam Syndrome" because they believe that the prosperity of the United States depends on successful interventions in defense of empire. Ordinary citizens, on the other hand, might find defense of empire at the expense of the poor to be in conflict with many of our stated values. Citizens must therefore be deceived into a defense of privilege through appeals to "freedom," "democracy," and the "threat of communism."

Low-intensity conflict is the present-day means through which the United States seeks to achieve generally unstated foreign-policy goals in the third world. Whereas the means for achieving certain objectives have evolved over time, the basic U.S. policy goals are essentially the same today as those stated in 1948 by George Kennan, who at the time headed the State Department's planning staff:

> . . . We have about 50% of the world's wealth, but only 6.3% of its populations. . . . In this situation, we cannot fail to be the object of envy and resentment. *Our real task in the coming period is to devise a pattern of relationships which will permit us to maintain this position of disparity without positive detriment to our national security.* To do so we have to dispense with all sentimentality and day-dreaming; and our attention will have to be concentrated everywhere on our immediate national objectives. We need not deceive ourselves that we can afford today the luxury of altruism and world-benefaction. . . . We should cease to talk about vague and . . . unreal objectives such as human rights, the raising of the living standards and democratization. The day is not far off when we are going to have to deal in straight power concepts. The less we are hampered by idealistic slogans, the better [italics added].[12]

Low-intensity conflict is the preferred strategy to achieve these goals into the next century. The true art of low-intensity warfare is its integration of "straight power concepts" with "ideological slogans" to cover up our defense of the Fifth Freedom, the right to rob and exploit. Kennan was both right and wrong. The challenge of empire is to maintain a "position of disparity" between ourselves and the poor "without positive detriment to our national security," but this can be achieved only by convincing the U.S. people of our noble intentions. "Idealistic slogans" far from being a hindrance are central to the defense of empire.

U.S. government officials who labeled Nicaragua a "totalitarian dungeon" and the contras "freedom fighters" knew that these were rhetorical abuses that trampled upon the truth. Rhetoric is not designed to serve the truth. It is calculated to serve political objectives. The contras were created by the U.S. government to inflict terror on civilians in service to U.S. political objectives. (I will discuss more fully the important role terrorism plays within low-intensity conflict in chap. 3, and U.S. efforts to create positive images for undemocratic forces it backs in chap. 4, below.) In order to understand why tiny countries like Nicaragua and El Salvador are seen as threats to the United States and how the United States confronts these threats, it is necessary to look more closely at the basic worldview that shapes low-intensity conflict.

BASIC WORLDVIEW

Low-intensity conflict can be understood only in the context of the philosophical foundations on which it is built. In the early 1980s peace movements in the United States and Western Europe were rapidly expanding. The U.S. political right countered this growing movement with a slogan and policy known as "peace through strength." The way to peace, according to the advocates of this position (which, not surprisingly, included the military and military contractors), is through massive military expenditures and greatly expanded nuclear and non-nuclear war-making capabilities.

The illusionary promise of "peace through strength" is that "peace" can be achieved while maintaining existing inequalities and without greater global justice or cooperation. The United States can guarantee the security of its "national valuables" by developing a sophisticated interventionist war-making capacity to protect itself from the poor throughout the third world and by constructing a technologically sophisticated nuclear shield around its own borders (known as Star Wars).

Low-intensity conflict is one component in a strategy to achieve "peace through strength." It is designed to protect U.S. interests throughout the third world. Its philosophy, which would make George Orwell proud, can be summarized as "peace through perpetual warfare." The way to peace is through constant interventionism.

The Council for Inter-American Security, in a paper commonly referred to as the Santa Fe Report, described and set the ideological and foreign-policy agenda for the Reagan administration. The report, which was written in 1980, states clearly the philosophical foundations for low-intensity conflict. "Foreign policy is the instrument by which peoples seek to assure their survival in a hostile world. War, not peace, is the norm of international affairs."[13] Peace, according to low-intensity-conflict planners, is a dangerous illusion. The United States is a country constantly at war and always under attack.

Traditional images of war and peace have failed to inspire citizen support for third-world interventionism. Low-intensity-conflict advocates insist, therefore, that the defense of U.S. security interests depends on a redefinition of what it means to be at war or at peace. A 1986 final report prepared by the "Joint Low-Intensity-Conflict Project [of the] United States Army Training and Doctrine Command" indicated that the country's major foreign-policy challenge was "how to defend threatened United States interests in conflict environments short of conventional war." In order to guarantee our security we needed to overcome "our perceptions that the nation and the world are either at war or at peace, with the latter being the normal state."[14]

Secretary of State George Shultz, in a speech to the Pentagon conference on low-intensity conflict in 1986, warned that war and peace are not distinct realities and to view them as such could threaten the security interests of the United States:

> We have seen and we will continue to see a wide range of ambiguous threats in the shadow area between major war and millennial peace. Americans must understand . . . that a number of small challenges, year after year, can add up to a more serious challenge to our interests. The time to act, to help our friends by adding our strength to the equation, is not when the threat is at our doorstep, when the stakes are highest and the needed resources enormous. We must be prepared to commit our political, economic, and, if necessary, military power when the threat is still manageable and when its prudent use can prevent the threat from growing.[15]

Another philosophical assumption of low-intensity conflict is that any social-change efforts not specifically controlled by the United States are the work of communists who are tools of Moscow or Cuba. "The young Caribbean republics situated in our strategic backyard face not only the natural growing pains of young nationhood," the Santa Fe Report states, "but the dedicated, irrepressible activity of a Soviet-backed Cuba to win ultimately total hegemony over this region. And this region . . . is the 'soft underbelly of the United States.' "[16]

Low-intensity-conflict proponents blame "communist subversion" for social turmoil in many different countries. No matter where the conflict is centered, it is always the United States that is under attack. This helps explain the interventionist thrust in Shultz's speech quoted above and the paranoia-riddled rhetoric of the Santa Fe Report.

Low-intensity conflict is the product of a worldview that sees any threat to perceived U.S. interests, no matter how small, as part of a global struggle with serious implications for the U.S. empire. A bipartisan report on Central America commissioned by the Reagan administration states this view clearly: "Beyond the issue of U.S. security interests in the Central American-Caribbean region, our credibility worldwide is engaged. The triumph of hostile forces . . . would be read as a sign of U.S. impotence."[17]

Low-intensity-conflict planners place all exploited third-world countries in one of two camps: either they are puppets of the Soviet Union or they are controlled assets of the United States. Nonalignment is a contradiction in terms. Third-world countries must either submit themselves to broad U.S. interference in their internal affairs, including granting the United States access to vital resources, military bases, and markets, or be targeted as enemies and threats to the national security of the United States. If they make the dignified choice of defending their rights to national sovereignty and pursuing economic policies that favor the interests of the poor, they will be subjected to low-intensity warfare. U.S. efforts to punish, destabilize, or overthrow disobedient governments by fomenting armed opposition against them is known as proinsurgency, an important component of low-intensity conflict.

The philosophy that shapes low-intensity conflict also excludes the possibility of indigenous, nationalistic revolutions in response to legitimate historical grievances. Any movement that arises against an oppressive U.S. client-state is seen as a communist-inspired and -directed attack against "vital U.S. interests." Third-world social-change movements seeking to build mixed economy or socialist alternatives to oppressive capitalist structures are seen as cogs in an international communist conspiracy. They are to be defeated through U.S.-backed counterinsurgency.

Another important philosophical component of low-intensity conflict is the belief that the United States is already losing World War III. "Survival demands a new U.S. foreign policy," the Santa Fe Report states. "America must seize the initiative or perish. For World War III is almost over."[18]

The use of World War III as an image to rally the U.S. people to the defense of empire is a good example of low-intensity conflict's philosophical view of the world and its ability to manipulate psychological images. World War III is a horrible prospect to most U.S. citizens who have some understanding of the destruction of previous global wars or who know something about the awesome power of nuclear weapons. Greater fear is elicited by telling us that this war against our formidable adversary, the Soviet Union, is already being lost. Our failure regularly to intervene and project power throughout the world "places the very existence of the Republic in peril." A more extensive quotation from the Santa Fe Report provides clues to understanding low-intensity conflict:

Foreign policy is the instrument by which peoples seek to assure their survival in a hostile world. War, not peace, is the norm in international affairs. For the United States of America, isolationism is impossible. Containment of the Soviet Union is not enough. Detente is dead. Survival demands a new U.S. foreign policy. America must seize the initiative or perish. For World War III is almost over. The Soviet Union, operating under the cover of increasing nuclear superiority, is strangling the Western industrialized nations. . . . Latin America and Southern Asia are the scenes of strife of the third phase of World War III. The first two phases — containment and detente — have been succeeded by the Soviet strategy of double envelopment — interdiction of the West's oil and ore and the geographical encirclement of the PRC [People's Republic of China]. America's basic freedoms and economic self interest require that the United States be and act as a first rate power.[19]

Low-intensity conflict redefines World War III while playing on traditional fears. Most U.S. citizens expect that if World War III is fought the Soviet Union will be our adversary. Low-intensity-conflict planners insist that this war is already underway and is global in scope. However, the strategic location of this war is now the third world, the enemy is the poor, and low-intensity conflict is the key to victory.

Low-intensity-conflict planners shift the strategic battleground to the third world because a nuclear or conventional war with the Soviets in Europe is regarded as too costly and therefore unlikely. It is possible in the coming years that the United States will pursue nuclear-arms reductions with the Soviet Union in order to free up resources for more sophisticated interventionism against the poor. Lieutenant General Samuel Wilson, former head of the Defense Intelligence Agency, states the logic of greater involvement in the third world in these terms:

There is little likelihood of a strategic nuclear confrontation with the Soviets. It is almost as unlikely that the Soviet Warsaw Pact forces will come tearing through the Fulda Gap in a conventional thrust. We live today with conflict of a different sort . . . and we had better get on with the ballgame.[20]

World War III is being fought at the edges of the empires, in the strategic third world where the "West's oil and ore" are to be found. What low-intensity-conflict planners refer to as World War III is in fact a U.S. war against the poor in the third world. Tiny Nicaragua and El Salvador suddenly take on an importance out of all proportion to their size or resources because, from the point of view of low-intensity conflict, they are central battlegrounds in this war.

World War III is not the only key concept to be used but redefined by low-intenstiy-conflict planners. The concept of total war has also been injected with new meaning. Traditionally total war has implied an all-out nuclear exchange between the superpowers. However, low-intensity conflict has been defined by Colonel John Waghelstein, commander of the army's Seventh Special Forces, as "total war at the grassroots level." Low-intensity conflict, according to Waghelstein, is more than a simple description of the levels of military violence; it is the integration of military aspects of warfare with "political, economic, and psychological warfare, with the military being a distant fourth in many cases."[21]

Low-intensity conflict is total war because it seeks to control all aspects of life. The United States is seeking to manage, control, or subvert social-change governments or movements throughout the third world through a unified warfare strategy that has economic, psychological, diplomatic, and military components. Low-intensity conflict is a totalitarianlike strategy. It seeks to control the hearts and minds, economic and political life of people while employing flexible military tactics.

THE REAL ENEMY

Any visitor to Central America will be shocked by the living conditions of the majority of people. Inadequate housing, malnutrition, limited access to health care or education, the lack of clean drinking water, unemployment or underemployment, high infant mortality and few channels for political participation accurately describe the situation of the majorities in many third-world countries. Political and economic power is in the hands of an unholy alliance of foreign-based multinational companies, internal economic elites, the military, and often the U.S. embassy.

Living conditions for the poor have worsened throughout the third world in recent years. More than 700 million people worldwide do not get enough food for an active and healthy life.[22] Each year 40 million people die from hunger and hunger-related diseases. This is equivalent to more than 300 jumbo jet crashes daily for a year in which there are no survivors and in which half of the victims are children.[23] Three-fifths of the population of underdeveloped countries and nearly half of the world population do not have access to safe and adequate drinking water. Each day more than 25,000 persons die for lack of clean drinking water. The World Health Organization estimates that 80 percent of all sickness and disease can be attributed to inadequate water and sanitation and that safe drinking water and sanitation could reduce infant mortality by 50 percent.[24]

Statistics may be useful in illustrating the magnitude of problems facing third-world peoples, but they say little or nothing about the human tragedies that lie behind such numbers, their structural causes, or the contributing role of U.S. policies. Low-intensity-conflict planners are counting on their ability to sell their worldview to the U.S. people, who have very little concrete experience of poverty and injustice in the third world. To U.S. citizens who have few personal ties to the people of Central America or limited experience in the third world, "freedom," "democracy," and "menacing communism" are likely to be powerful images that elicit uncritical nationalistic impulses.

It is impossible to imagine 40 million people dying in plane crashes each year without individuals, companies, and governments seriously questioning the basic soundness of airplane construction, maintenance, and the systems of traffic control. When it comes to the international economy, however, individuals, groups, or governments that challenge the premises of the present capitalist international order are labeled communists. Third-world countries or social-change movements that seek to change domestic or international priorities in order to enhance the power and position of the poor are subjected to low-intensity warfare.

I have written elsewhere in more detail about the political and economic causes of hunger and poverty.[25] Here I intend to give a brief summary of key issues in order to provide a context for an analysis of low-intensity conflict as a war against the poor.

The poor throughout the third world are generally victims of dual injustices. Neither the international economy nor their internal economies are structured to meet their needs. Land and other productive resources remain concentrated in the hands of relatively small minorities. Credit is controlled by and targeted to the rich, and foreign-exchange earnings are squandered in luxury consumption. Land-use is geared to the production of coffee, bananas, beef, fruits, vegetables, and other export crops for foreign markets. The upper and middle classes ensure adequate nutrition by relying on imported foods, but the emphasis on export agriculture, together with a lack of access to productive land, makes hunger a daily companion to the poor. Many of the rural poor are seasonal workers on plantations owned by others. Unable to subsist without land or with meager wages, they are pushed into the cities where jobs are scarce and misery is all too common.

The economic situation described above is in large part a product of elite control of third-world economies and the fact that the rich throughout the third world have built important political, military, and economic alliances with their counterparts in developed countries. They are more concerned about their role within the international economy than about the well-being of the majority of their citizens.

The integration of poor-country economies into the international market victimizes the poor who by definition lack the purchasing power necessary to direct production and distribution of goods to meet their needs. The global farms, factories, and supermarkets that make up the world economy generate transnational alliances among the relatively powerful while further marginalizing the poor. Third-world-country elites, for example, need not implement structural reforms that would redistribute wealth and expand domestic markets because they buy and sell in an international market.

The groups that manage global production are motivated by profits to be made in servicing and expanding the consumer desires of the relatively affluent. The agenda of the poor is ignored and, if the demands of the poor become an obstacle to the Fifth Freedom, they are repressed through low-intensity conflict.

The economies of most third-world countries are highly dependent on outside industrial powers, which supply them with capital, technology, and markets. Present-day dependency is historically rooted in the period of colonial domination. Colonial economies served outside interests while giving rise to internal sectors that had a stake in economic arrangements that benefited them while impoverishing the majority. With the coming of political independence, colonial trade gave way to the "free international market" without altering the unequal power relationships that are the root of poverty and dependency.

The ongoing dependency of third-world countries generates conflict between unequal actors in the international arena. Poor-country elites remain largely subservient to their counterparts in developed countries. The conflicts generated by dependency can be seen today in relation to the deteriorating terms of trade. Dependency is a consequence of a lack of power to influence the international economy. After twenty-five years of clamoring for fairer terms of trade and a New International Economic Order (NIEO), the prices poor countries receive for their traditional agricultural and mineral exports continue to fall relative to the costs of essential imports. For example, the prices paid for third-world raw commodities hit their lowest levels in history in 1986, relative to the prices of manufactured goods and services.[26]

One consequence of unjust terms of trade is greater dependency in the form of indebtedness. The United States and other industrial countries have repeatedly refused to redistribute economic wealth and power by changing the rules of the international trading game. The substitution of limited aid and credit for fair international pricing has resulted in a skyrocketing debt burden among third-world countries. One indication of the weak trade position of third-world countries is that their debt burden has grown in a parallel manner with the expansion of world trade. The value of world trade expanded from U.S. $60 billion in 1950 to $2 trillion in 1980.[27] In the mid-1960s third-world-country debt was approximately $40 billion. By 1988, according to a specialist at the World Bank, poor-country indebtedness reached $1.2 trillion. In 1987, after factoring in aid received, the so-called developing countries exported more than $27 billion to the developed world, mostly in the form of interest payments.[28]

Yearly principle and interest payments for third-world countries have more than quadrupled in the decade of the 1980s. The third world pays out annually in principle and interest payments nearly three times more money than it receives in aid from all developed-country governments and international aid agencies combined. "To accumulate funds to pay these debts—or at least part of them," a special report from OXFAM America states, "many Third World governments are squeezing every available bit of wealth from already weak economies. The sources of wealth they are tapping are underground mineral, tropical forests, fertile land, and the labor of factory workers and farmers."[29]

Luis Ignacio da Silva, a Brazilian trade union leader, draws on the image of World War III in the context of the debt crisis:

> I tell you that the Third World War has already started — a silent war, not for that reason any less sinister. This war is tearing down Brazil, Latin America, and practically all of the Third World. Instead of soldiers there are children dying, instead of destruction of bridges there is the tearing down of factories, hospitals, and entire economies. . . . It is a war by the United States against the Latin American continent and the Third World. It is a war over the foreign debt, a war which has as its main weapon interest, a weapon more deadly than the atom bomb, more shattering than a laser beam.[30]

The greatest moral scandal of our time is *death through international finance.* Although we rightfully find the Holocaust in Nazi Germany to be an affront to all decency, we quietly tolerate the death of far greater numbers of people each year as a result of the international debt crisis, which is saddled on the backs of the poor. OXFAM America's report, "Third World Debt: Payable in Hunger," states:

> The burden of paying the Third World's debts has fallen most heavily on those least able to carry it — the poor. Workers in the cities and peasants in the countryside are being pressed to produce more and consume less to help their countries try to earn their way out of debt.
>
> . . . [T]he International Monetary Fund [along with governments, private banks, and other multinational lending agencies such as the World Bank] nearly always requires indebted countries to promise to implement "Adjustment Programs." . . .
>
> One intent of Adjustment Programs within the indebted countries is to reduce consumption of all kinds of goods and services. The IMF calls this "demand management." It is meant to ensure that more of the debtor nation's resources will be used to produce exports to be sold for dollars that can then be used to pay debts.
>
> Among the conditions typically required . . . are cuts in public spending — which often mean fewer health and education services — and elimination of government subsidies used to keep food prices low. . . .
>
> *Adjustment Programs usually result in increases in the cost of food, clothing, kerosene, bus fares, fertilizers and other goods needed by farmers and the poor. They are the hardest on the most vulnerable people* [italics added].[31]

CONCLUSION

Under the cover of rhetoric about "freedom," "democracy," and fighting the "communist menace," the United States is waging a war against the poor and in defense of privilege and empire. Low-intensity conflict is a term that refers to any challenge to U.S. privileges throughout the third world short of conventional or nuclear war. Low-intensity conflict is also the strategy of warfare through which the United States seeks to maintain a system in which death through international finance is the norm, and poor people — not poverty — is the enemy. The United States could place its formidable resources and strength at the service of overcoming the structural causes of poverty. However, to do so would involve a major rethinking of who we are as a people, a reassessment of national priorities, a willingness to express national repentance, and a commitment to share both resources and power.

2

The "Crimes" of the Poor

U.S. foreign policy must begin to counter . . . liberation theology as it is utilized in Latin America by the "liberation theology" clergy. . . . Unfortunately, Marxist-Leninist forces have utilized the church as a political weapon against private property and productive capitalism by infiltrating the religious community with ideas that are less Christian than communist.

Santa Fe Report

By a miracle I am able to tell you the story of my grand crime for which they threatened me with death. They took my son who was 18 years old, shot him, peeled off his skin and cut him into pieces. Then they hung him from a cross in a tree. They cut his testicles off and put them in his mouth. They did this to warn me because I was a celebrator of the word of God. That was my crime. . . . We had to leave because they persecuted the whole land.

Our crime is to be poor and ask for bread. Here the laws only favor the rich. However, the great majority of people are poor. Those who have jobs are exploited daily in the factories and on the farms. Without land we cannot plant. There is no work. This brings more hunger, more misery. We are without clothes, schools or jobs. And so we demonstrate. But to speak of justice is to be called a communist, to ask for bread is subversive. It is a war of extermination. . . . It is a crime to be a Christian and to demand justice.

Salvadoran Campesino and Delegate of the Word, April 1988

INTRODUCTION

On a hot, steamy day in June 1987 I made my way to the office of El Salvador's Non-Governmental Human Rights Commission. The air was choked with smog from an endless stream of cars, buses, and burning garbage. San Salvador was still cluttered with rubble from October's earthquake, leaving the impression of a city under seige.

The political atmosphere was equally disquieting. The United States had spent several billion dollars since 1980 on its low-intensity-conflict project for El Salvador. The project had a wide range of components, which corresponded to the needs of each political moment. These components included the use of massive or selective terror, brutal bombing of civilians followed by military involvement in distribution of aid, and the election of a president from the Christian Democratic Party. U.S.-sponsored elections had provided a democratic façade designed to cover up major injustices.

The veneer of democracy in El Salvador was unraveling at the time of my June visit. In May the Lutheran church, which is doing important work with both war and earthquake victims, was taken over by armed gunmen. The intruders took lists of names of church members and donors. The same month the offices of the Mothers of the Disappeared were bombed and several members of the Non-Governmental Human Rights Commission received death threats. The atmosphere was tense as growing numbers of Salvadorans defied the subtle and not so subtle repression and took to the streets demanding deeper economic reforms, authentic democracy, and an end to the U.S.-backed war. Government security forces regularly videotaped these demonstrations. In a country where, despite U.S. rhetoric to the contrary, the death squads had never been dismantled, such actions were meant to intimidate and to sow terror.

A modest middle-class home had been converted for use as offices for the Human Rights Commission. There were no outside markings to identify the commission. This was a reminder of the daily yet unreported terror that shapes life in El Salvador. Sign or no sign, the feared Cherokee jeeps that are identified with death squads and disappearances patrolled the streets in front of the offices.

I entered the office through the kitchen where a few dirty coffee cups sat in the sink. A series of photographs looked out from the walls of the hallway leading to a living room. Other photographs lined the living-room wall itself. Photo albums sat on a coffee table in the center of the room. It was a welcoming scene that would have been familiar in many U.S. homes, except that the pictures were not of smiling family members but of mutilated corpses and tortured bodies of men, women, and children. The pictures nauseated me and yet they were similar to scenes I had witnessed while living in Nicaragua where the U.S.-backed contras terrorized civilians.

The photos in the Human Rights office reminded me of personal testimonies I had heard from dozens of mothers who, like many hundreds of thousands of Salvadorans, had been brutalized and displaced in the U.S.-backed war. Many described how government security forces had come to their villages, ripped babies from their mother's wombs or arms and used them for target practice. Their experiences and my own in Nicaragua had taught me that low-intensity conflict was capable of inflicting high-intensity emotional and physical pain.

The anguished photographs and personal stories reminded me of the New Testament image of the body of Christ and how, as members of one body, we are to rejoice or suffer together. I thought too of my wife, Sara, at the time pregnant with our daughter, Hannah. In God's eyes, I reminded myself, the death of each of these nameless people is no less important than my own death or those of my loved ones, or the death of Jesus.

Christians who live in the United States are intimately tied to the hope and pain of the Salvadoran people. Our common faith should require us to understand and enter into their crucifixion. This is particularly true because we are bound together not only through faith but through our tax dollars that pay for their suffering. Congress provided more than $1.5 million daily in FY 1987 to bankroll the U.S. war against the poor in El Salvador. The U.S. low-intensity-conflict project in El Salvador received widespread support from both Republicans and Democrats, who described a country at war against its own people as an exemplary democracy.

El Salvador is a tiny country far from the consciousness of most U.S. citizens. It, along with Nicaragua, is considered "an ideal testing ground" for low-intensity-conflict doctrine.[1] The "crimes of the poor" manifest themselves clearly here, and the U.S. judges them harshly.

Herbert Anaya, president of the Non-Governmental Human Rights Commission, spoke to me that June day about the U.S. war against the poor in his country, about low-intensity conflict, human rights, and human hope. He spoke with the passion of one who loved his people to the point of giving his life. As I listened and felt the power of his words I scribbled into the margin of my notebook, "I am talking to a dead man." His words, quoted extensively below, offer clues for an understanding of the "crimes of the poor" and low-intensity conflict's response to those "crimes."

THE LIVING WORDS OF A MARTYR

On Monday, October 27, 1987, Herbert Ernesto Anaya was killed by two men firing handguns with silencers as he left his home to drive two of his six children to school. The words I had written anticipating his death convicted and haunted me. When I awoke to hear the news of his death, I knew that I had killed him. I, along with many others, had failed to reach the conscience of the U.S. people. Most U.S. citizens had never heard the term "low-intensity conflict." They remained indifferent to U.S. policies that impose suffering on the people of El Salvador, Nicaragua, and throughout much of the third world.

Herbert Anaya's courageous words, now sealed with blood, continue to convict us and to offer us hope:

The social reality of El Salvador is complicated. Human rights are part of that social reality. It is the lack of basic needs that most violates human rights. It is this lack that has generated discontent and given rise to war. Our organization like others searches for peace by seeking to eliminate the causes that perpetuate war in El Salvador. . . .

The basic question in El Salvador today is whether or not the human rights situation is improving. The situation of human rights . . . corresponds to the historical development of popular movements. As hunger intensifies and housing deteriorates the people make organized demands and these demands are met with repression. In other words, repression grows in response to the strength of popular organizations. Whatever changes in El Salvador's human rights situation must be understood in social terms as part of [the U.S.] counterinsurgency strategy. Human rights are weighed in light of political gains.

There is talk of democracy in El Salvador, but the government's "respect for human rights" is a tactic to deepen the war. When they [the U.S. embassy and El Salvadoran government] speak of peace they mean war; when they speak of respect for human rights they mean violation of human rights. They talk about the "reappearance" of the death squads, but the death squads never disappeared. Shifting patterns of human rights violations respond to the needs of the psychological war.

The intelligence services of the army are death squads. They operate in civilian clothes. Now the popular organizations are increasing and so the groundwork is being laid to justify a new wave of repression. The government says it's not involved with death squads, but they are from within the security system. They say behind all the problems there is communism. People are accused in this way and they are disappeared, killed, and tortured.

It doesn't cost anything for them to talk of democracy. They speak of freedom and arrest the people; they speak of the rights of workers while persecuting them; they talk about "humanizing the conflict" while inflicting more and more suffering. You have to know and feel it. Low-intensity conflict brings misery and suffering. The period coming will be accompanied by enormous repression. We are not prophets but the repression caused by the social situation is already in motion. . . .

We are persecuted in an effort to prevent us from documenting cases [of human rights abuses] and speaking out. They justify our persecution by saying we are collaborators with the guerrillas. The goal is to discredit all independent organizations. . . . The U.S. embassy doesn't talk to us anymore. The U.S. embassy is in agreement with our destruction. We are a thorn to be eliminated. This month two pickup trucks with armed civilians have come to our offices. Today, we have received anonymous calls threatening us with death. . . .

The Salvadoran government and the U.S. embassy speak about quantitative improvements in human rights. They see reductions in numbers as progress. However, repression is part of a political moment. Through past repression they cut off the head of the popular movements. In 1983, for example, they decided to achieve their goal and the massive terror had its effect. After destroying the popular movements they began talking about "respecting human rights." The psychological terror is repression with a purpose. It is part of a political tactic, part of counterinsurgency. Today poverty and injustice are giving rise once again to the people's movements and so now we are moving from selective repression back to massive terror. It is considered time to "turn the screws." The security forces are being given a freer hand. The present moment is very dangerous.

The only solution to El Salvador's problems is economic and social change that eliminates the causes of the war. In the military there are 65,000 soldiers. More than 35,000 civilians must participate in civil defense. Through the government's counterinsurgency campaign "United to Reconstruct," the people are given a few things and then told to fight the guerrillas. Our external debt is enormous, as is our governmental budget deficit. The economic crisis is worsening with talk of another devaluation coming as a condition of continued U.S. aid. Inflation and hunger both grow. . . .

We experience constant persecution. Whatever political space we have has been achieved with our blood. The same is true for unions and cooperatives. If we live, we live with the clear understanding that many of us have the possibility of disappearance and death hanging over our heads. They can't tear out our convictions. They can't bribe us with money or guarantees of personal security, which they offered to us in prison.

Military uniforms involved in civic actions are stained with the people's blood. Hunger will not be solved through handouts but through social transformation. Repression will prolong not resolve the crisis. Whatever germ of inequality is planted also nourishes the seed of social injustice and the determination to transform the society. With our final breath we will continue our work. This isn't heroism. It is simply doing what we have to do. [At this point in my notes is etched: "I am talking to a dead man."]

Poor people are dying. The government doesn't care about poor people. . . . People don't want war, but war is the reality here. War will not be humanized. If the war goes on, the death will go on. The war will never bring about the triumph of one force over another. That is why dialogue is so important.

LESSONS FROM ANAYA

In chapter 3, below, I will examine more fully the actual means by which the United States wages war in response to the "crimes of the poor." Here

I want to consider several observations about the nature of these "crimes" and the U.S. response to them in light of Anaya's analysis.

First, the poor become criminals if they speak out and organize to change the causes of their poverty. Receiving handouts is acceptable; social transformation is not. Poor people and poor nations who passively accept their situation are not guilty of any crime.

Second, it is a crime to be an independent person, organization, or nation.

Third, it is a crime to defend fundamental human rights, including the right to food, work, shelter, land, health care, and other basic needs.

Fourth, it is a crime to seek a negotiated settlement to the political and economic crisis that would include sharing power with the poor.

Fifth, it is a crime to raise questions about or seek alternatives to capitalism even though there is abundant evidence of the misery caused by the present order. Any alternative is seen as part of a communist conspiracy.

Sixth, U.S. and Salvadoran policies treat poor people as criminals while minimizing the problem of poverty. The goal of such policies is to *control* the poor, not to overcome the structural causes of poverty, which in fact low-intensity-conflict strategy seeks to maintain.

Seventh, the U.S. embassy and the Salvadoran government manage repression. The goal is to use the appropriate amount of physical and psychological terror necessary to maintain control and intimidate the poor.

Eighth, the United States punishes the "crimes of the poor" by waging a criminal war against the poor. The U.S. low-intensity-conflict project utilizes a variety of means to maintain control and discourage or punish the "crimes of the poor." These methods include severe or targeted repression, imprisonment or disappearance of wrongdoers, bribes or offers of personal security, death threats and actual assassinations, massive bombing of civilians, handouts of food and other goods in exchange for participation in civil defense programs, campaigns to discredit independent organizations, red-baiting, and conditioning aid to the Salvadoran government on policies desired by the United States such as devaluation of the Salvadoran currency.

Ninth, U.S. policies create and manage images in order to obscure reality. Elections are held and democracy is talked about, but power remains in the hands of the U.S. embassy and Salvadoran elites. Human rights violations measured as a body count are fewer, but intimidation remains constant and the structures of repression are maintained. Death squads "disappear" without ever having left the scene. Just as the enemy is defined as poor people and not poverty, so too images and not reality are altered.

OFFENDING THE EMPIRE

The U.S. war against the poor is a war against hope. Hope is the enemy of empires because it is hope that gives rise to alternative futures. Desperation in the form of hunger and poverty is more likely to crush people's spirits than to give rise to resistance. A desperate or near desperate situation injected with hope, on the other hand, makes empires nervous. Nicaraguan poet Edwin Castro was killed in 1960 in a jail of the U.S.-backed Somoza dictatorship. His poem "Tomorrow," written from his cell, captured and fueled the hope of the Nicaraguan people whose revolution was born out of the capacity to envision an alternative future:

The daughter of the worker, the daughter of the peasant, won't have to prostitute herself—bread and work will come from her honorable labor.

No more tears in the homes of workers. You'll stroll happily over the laughter of paved roads, bridges, country lanes. . . .

Tomorrow, my son, everything will be different; no whips, jails, bullets, rifles will repress ideas. You'll stroll through the streets of all the cities with the hands of your children in your hands—as I cannot do with you.

Jail will not shut in your young years as it does mine; and you will not die in exile with your eyes trembling, longing for the landscape of your homeland, like my father died. Tomorrow, my son, everything will be different.

I had many conversations with poor campesinos in Central America which reinforce how the U.S. war against the poor is fundamentally a war to destroy the capacity to hope, envision, and work for an alternative future. When I questioned campesinos in Mexico and Honduras many would stare at their feet in silence. After several moments they would respond without confidence. Their answers would often be prefaced with degrading phrases such as "We are stupid, ignorant poeple who know nothing" or "We are like oxen who know nothing."

The internalization of oppression and poverty is encouraged and welcomed by empires. It is the product of centuries of economic exploitation coupled with a degrading theology that stresses poverty as God's will, obedience to church and secular authority, and heavenly rewards.

Organized campesinos in El Salvador and Nicaragua, by way of contrast, generally spoke with clarity, dignity, and hope. In El Salvador, despite repression and the formidable power of the United States, they believed they could alter their history of landlessness and oppression through organization and struggle. In Nicaragua the people had begun living a different future when they made the decision to participate actively in the movement to overthrow the U.S.-backed Somoza dictatorship. They had tasted the fruit of their hope, the promise of Edwin Castro's "Tomorrow," after the triumph of their revolution in 1979.

The United States escalated its war against hope in response to the success of the Nicaraguan revolution. Nicaraguan President Daniel Ortega, in a speech on the fifth anniversary of the triumph of the Nicaraguan people, offers this poetic description of how hope kindled the wrath of the U.S. empire:

> Five years ago the song of the roosters and birds heralded the triumph of the reign of dreams and of hope. Five years ago the church bells and rifle and machine gunfire resounded announcing the news: the birth of the free people of Nicaragua. And all of Nicaragua began to write the most beautiful poem. . . .
>
> But these verses disturbed the snoring of Goliath, Goliath who had stolen our voice and shackled our country. These verses annoyed Goliath as he saw David standing tall, since he thought he had killed him when he killed Sandino. Then Goliath hurled himself once again at David, that is, against the workers, the peasants, against the young people and women, against children, against the heroic people of Nicaragua.[2]

Ortega's use of biblical imagery to describe U.S. attacks against his people illustrates why the Santa Fe Report targets liberation theology as enemy. Liberation theology grows out of the experiences of oppressed peoples. Common people, as well as trained theologians, reflect upon the meaning of Scripture in light of the oppression of the poor and their longing for freedom. In both El Salvador and Nicaragua, liberation theology has been instrumental in awakening people's hope. The "crime" of the Delegate of the Word quoted at the beginning of this chapter is that he celebrated faith in a God who proclaims "good news to the poor," "freedom to the captives" and "liberation to the oppressed." Celebrating this God is a "criminal activity" because it shatters centuries of psychological and physical oppression by offering to the poor hope for a better future. God takes sides with the poor in their struggle for liberation.

A liberating God is upsetting to the traditional gods called upon by empires, autocrats, and oligarchs to justify unjust privileges and to stifle the hopes of the poor. Jeane Kirkpatrick, former U.S. ambassador to the United Nations, offers this defense of U.S. support for regimes that victimize the poor:

> Traditional autocrats leave in place existing allocations of wealth, power, status, and other resources which in most traditional societies favor an affluent few and maintain masses in poverty. But they worship traditional gods and observe traditional taboos. They do not disturb the habitual rhythms of work and leisure, habitual places of residence, habitual patterns of family and personal relations. Because the miseries of traditional life are familiar, they are bearable to ordinary people who, growing up in the society, learn to cope.[3]

Liberation theology is part of a "criminal conspiracy" because it doesn't help poor people cope with inhuman conditions and social systems that "favor an affluent few and maintain masses in poverty." It calls both rich and poor people to a faithful response to the liberating gospel of Jesus Christ. This gospel challenges the structures of death and calls people to new life. The traditional gods of oligarchy and empire have, in the words of Walter Brueggemann, a "royal consciousness [which] leads to numbness, especially to numbness about death. It is the task of prophetic ministry and imagination to bring people to engage their experiences of suffering to death."[4]

The Santa Fe Report targets liberation theology as a major challenge to U.S. foreign policy because *it refuses to be silent about death or about the possibilities for new life*. Liberation theology challenges the gods of the empire and the empire itself. It provides the spiritual food for communities of exploited people who examine "their experiences of suffering to death" in light of structural causes and the liberating example of Jesus Christ.

Poverty, far from being sanctioned by God, is a scandalous affront to a loving God. It is a consequence of human injustice built into unjust social structures. The poor will not be judged by their obedience to authority and their quiet endurance of earthly misery but are free to be faithful to a God that works for liberation within history, as the Pharaoh unhappily discovered. The rich are not wealthy because they are blessed by God but because they exploit the poor. The poor are not oxenlike workers ordained to be subservient to the rich but dignified human beings created in the image of God. Politics and economics do not lie outside the parameters of faith but are arenas in which Christians seek to live out their faith in a God that works for the redemption of all creation. The fruit of faith is not the pacifying promise of heavenly streets paved with gold but partial realizations of God's kingdom here and now through struggle and community. Jesus is not a passive victim who died as part of a preordained plan of God to overcome abstract sin, but an example of a faithful follower of a liberating God who challenged the empire of his time and lived out his faith and convictions to the ultimate consequence.[5]

The hope that springs from a theology of liberation encourages the "crimes of the poor." Hope is dangerous and the empire in self-defense lashes out against it. Positive examples that might inspire hope in others are also enemies to be pressured, co-opted and, if necessary, destroyed.

THE "CRIMES" OF NICARAGUA

Miguel D'Escoto, Maryknoll priest and foreign minister of Nicaragua, in February 1986 began a 200-mile nonviolent march from the Honduran border to Nicaragua's capital city. The fifteen-day walk was a religious commemoration of the passion of Jesus and a reenactment of the traditional stations of the cross within Catholicism. It was also a prayerful attempt by D'Escoto, who earlier had fasted for more than thirty days, to call on religious people throughout the world to protest the crucifixion of the Nicaraguan people at the hands of the U.S. empire.

I walked with D'Escoto and many thousands of other Nicaraguans for
some of those fifteen days. We walked, sang, prayed, and talked. I heard
hundreds of personal stories of passion and crucifixion from people who
had experienced in the flesh of their own families and communities the
terror, torture, rape, and murder that accompanied attacks by U.S.-backed
contras. Each day of the march D'Escoto's words became more prophetic.
Speaking in front of the earthquake-damaged cathedral in Managua on the
final day of the march, he spoke of the "crimes" of the Nicaraguan people,
which had provoked the criminal wrath of the empire:

> The Lord wants it to be absolutely clear that if we are attacked, if we
> have provoked the criminal and bloody wrath of the Empire, it is for
> exactly the same reason that Jesus provoked that wrath. And it was
> for the same reason that so many innocents were killed when Christ
> was born, and that later Christ was taken to the cross.... It is not
> that we Nicaraguans are perfect but we have taken on the obligation
> as Christians to make a new society. We have worked for the advent
> of the kingdom, and this necessarily and inevitably raises the ire, the
> hate, the reprisals of those with established interests in maintaining
> the old order.

The Nicaraguan revolution is not perfect, but its imperfections had little
or nothing to do with the U.S. low-intensity-conflict project to destroy this
tiny nation. Most of the common charges leveled against the Nicaraguan
revolution (it is totalitarian, it exports arms to forment revolution in neighboring countries, it is a Soviet/Cuban puppet state, it will allow Soviet
military bases on its soil, it represses the church, it persecutes Jews, it
commits genocide against its native peoples, etc.) are easily refutable. It is
likely that these charges, which conform to the worldview described in the
previous chapter, are sincerely believed by some U.S. low-intensity-conflict
planners. However, it is equallly likely that these charges are intentionally
used by others who understand that they are clearly distorted but useful.
They provide a smokescreen that obscures the real reasons for U.S. hostility
toward Nicaragua: the poor cannot be allowed to break away from U.S.
control and take charge of their own resources and destiny.

Readers wanting a more detailed refutation of these charges or a more
in-depth description of the Nicaraguan revolution can look elsewhere.[6] Here
I will limit myself to a brief description of key philosophical and practical
components of the Nicaraguan revolution in order to explain why Nicaragua
is in fact dangerous to elite U.S. interests. This will pave the way for chapter
3, below, where I will examine how low-intensity-conflict strategy has been
implemented in Central America as part of the U.S. war against the poor.

The Nicaraguan revolution grew out of a long history of oppression and
U.S. domination. The fabric of the revolution is creatively woven together
using threads of nationalism, Christianity, and Marxist analysis. Its philo-

sophical base includes commitments to nonalignment, political pluralism, a mixed economy, and popular participation.

Nicaragua's strategy of nonalignment and mixed economy is based on a belief that greater independence is possible to the degree that Nicaragua is able to diversify its economic and political relationships. It has actively sought close ties to third-world nations, Western Europe and Canada, and the socialist bloc countries — and it would like normalized relations with the United States. Its mixed economy involves a conscious effort to diversify sources of trade and aid. It also guarantees within its constitution a role for cooperatives; joint state and private enterprises; small, medium, and large private farms and businesses; indigenous communal ownership; and a state sector. Numerous parties vie for political power in Nicaragua's elections. The revolution also encourages the people to organize themselves to shape the society and to improve living standards through participation in vaccination campaigns, adult education programs, harvesting brigades, and other neighborhood organizations.

These philosophical principles obviously collide with the worldview of low-intensity-conflict planners for whom nonalignment is a contradiction in terms, and a mixed economy is an attack against corporate capitalism. *Nicaragua's greatest "crime," however, is that it redistributes wealth from the rich to the poor*. It seeks to reorder society in order to reflect the interests and needs of the poor majority.

The Nicaraguan revolution's fundamental concern for the long-exploited poor was demonstrated through priority programs that improved literacy, education, and health care. In the first few years of the revolution, illiteracy was reduced from more than 50 percent to approximately 12 percent, successful preventive health programs including vaccinations led the World Health Organization to select Nicaragua as one of five model countries for primary health care, and infant mortality was reduced by one-third.

These social improvements were coupled with and ultimately dependent upon a restructuring of the economy to reflect the needs of the majorities. Steps were taken to redistribute wealth and wealth-producing resources from elites to the poor. Agrarian reform programs distributed land to campesinos free of charge and banks were nationalized so that credit could be widely distributed. In order to counter the common third-world problem of tax evasion by the rich, the Nicaraguan government nationalized the export-import trade, which gave it control of a large share of foreign-exchange earnings that traditionally had been used by the rich for luxury consumption. By requiring producers of agricultural export crops to sell to the government and paying them primarily with local currency, the government gained access to crucial dollars that could be used to finance development.

These mechanisms through which the Nicaraguan government worked to overcome a long legacy of poverty and exploitation offended the empire and its allies within Nicaragua, who immediately launched their war against the poor. Brazilian Bishop Pedro Casaldáliga, who joined Miguel D'Escoto during part of his lengthy fast, writes:

> I can understand how the revolution cannot be very pleasing to the landholders since it took away the land they had piled up. Just as it can't be very pleasant for the gringos, since the revolution messed up their fat profiteering. . . . Spanish greed, English greed, American greed, one after another—always oligarchical greed. It's about time that the rivers of Latin America, the peoples of Latin America, be freed of these greeds.[7]

The problem Nicaragua poses for the United States goes well beyond the limited resources at stake in a tiny, impoverished country of 3 million people. The "crimes of Nicaragua" have global implications. Ironically, the fact that Nicaragua is a poor, impoverished country makes it a greater danger to U.S. security interests. If a tiny, resource-poor country like Nicaragua is able to make significant improvements in the living standards of its people after partially freeing itself from the clutches of an empire, then this will undoubtedly fill others with hope. Impoverished people living in countries where far greater resources are now at the disposal of the empire are likely to be encouraged by Nicaragua's example. This is the context in which the quotation from George Shultz's speech to a Pentagon conference on low-intensity conflict, cited in chapter 1, above, can be understood:

> Americans must understand . . . that a number of small challenges, year after year, can add up to a more serious challenge to our interests. . . . We must be prepared to commit our political, economic, and, if necessary, military power when the threat is still manageable and when its prudent use can prevent the threat from growing.[8]

The final words in this chapter are from Herbert Anaya. His words to the U.S. people about their country's policies in El Salvador are equally relevant for Nicaragua:

> We feel you should know that each bomb ripping into our mountains and plains, destroying ranches, fields and human bodies, comes from your Army, sent as "aid" to the Salvadoran government. Our country has been converted into a proving ground for experimental political, military, economic and ideological projects developed in the White House and the Pentagon. Your government has become the center of domination and subjugation of poor peoples of the world: peoples with a unsatisfied hunger for justice, a deep thirst for a better and more humane future, and an unquenchable yearning for life. In each heart lies the certain hope, growing like a baby giant, of building peace with justice.

3

Low-Intensity Conflict:
The Strategy

I think the U.S. government enjoys playing with the stomachs of humanity.

A Nicaraguan Mother

It takes relatively few people and little support to disrupt the internal peace and economic stability of a small country.

William Casey, CIA Director

Four health workers were taken from their homes by the contras, then killed and their bodies mutilated. Three were Castilblanco brothers who worked with CEPAD, a Protestant relief and development agency: Nestor, father of two and administrator of CEPAD's local health program; Daniel; and Filemon. The fourth, Jesus Barrera, was a social worker with the Catholic church. Daniel's body was found with one eye missing, and Jesus was castrated. Before leaving town the contras burned down Daniel's house and stole the medicine from CEPAD's clinic. Daniel's wife had just given birth that day, and is left a widow with a newborn infant, whose home is destroyed.

Witness for Peace Report, 1986

INTRODUCTION

Living standards in Central America declined dramatically throughout the 1980s. Ongoing structural inequalities, declining terms of trade, and U.S. sponsored militarization of the region took a brutal toll, particularly on the poor. Nicaragua was especially hard hit by declining prices for its exports and the U.S.-imposed low-intensity war. By 1988, Nicaragua's econ-

27

omy was in shambles, with production down and inflation nearly uncontrollable. Rising food prices, crowded buses, and widespread shortages were evident throughout the country.

The stakes in Nicaragua are very high. It would be easy to conclude, as U.S. low-intensity-conflict planners would like, that the revolution has failed. The reality is more complex. Tiny Nicaragua's independence from the U.S. empire and the empire's response to that freedom placed Nicaragua on a bloodstained geopolitical stage. The seeds of hope that sprouted in Nicaragua spread light to impoverished people throughout the third world. The empire's response cast an ominous shadow. "We must proclaim that there are no geostrategic interests of the U.S. in Central America," states the Jesuit director of Nicaragua's Catholic University, "that can justify the financing of the death of the poor through the maintenance of ... counterrevolutionary war."[1]

Brazilian Bishop Pedro Casaldáliga underscores the broader significance of events unfolding in Nicaragua when he writes that "the United States should understand that the cause of Nicaragua is the cause of all Latin America. . . . I believe that Nicaragua's cause is also the cause of the whole church of Jesus."[2]

U.S. strategists hope to limit our vision of Nicaragua to obvious problems such as food shortages, rising prices, and crowded buses. They work to distort our view of the *causes* of these problems and they hope to obscure the direct relationship that exists between implementation of low-intensity-conflict strategy and widespread suffering in Nicaragua.

U.S. policymakers may or may not succeed in overthrowing the Nicaraguan revolution. However, even if successful they will never be able to claim ultimate victory in their war against the poor unless we fall into the trap of looking at history through the policymakers' distorted lenses. "In this world of betrayal," Salvadoran poet Ramon del Campoamor writes, "there is nothing true or false. Everything depends on the color of the crystal through which one gazes."

LESSONS FROM THE PAST: BASIC BACKGROUND

The Vietnam War was the most costly and deadly third-world intervention in U.S. history. U.S. bombers saturated Vietnam with more than 7 million tons of bombs, nearly three times the combined totals from the Korean and Second World wars. More than 6.5 million Vietnamese, approximately the combined populations of Minnesota and Iowa, were killed or injured during the years 1965 through 1974. Most of the victims were civilians.

The suffering caused by the U.S. intervention was not limited to the people of Indochina. The war tore apart the emotional and economic fabric of the United States. More than 3 million U.S. soliders were deployed in Vietnam. U.S. casualties numbered more than 360,000, with approximately

50,000 deaths. Protests spread from college campuses and churches into the main streets of cities across the United States. The Vietnam War also accelerated the militarization of the U.S. economy. This trend continued throughout the post-Vietnam period to the point that "if the U.S. military industry were a national economy, it would be the 13th largest in the world."[3] Military priorities have seriously distorted both the U.S. and the global economy.

Poor people in the United States suffered directly and indirectly as a result of the U.S. involvement in Vietnam. They fought and died in disproportionate numbers in a racist war that defended elite class interests. Also, President Lyndon Johnson's Great Society programs that were to improve living standards for the poor were undermined by the escalating costs of the war against the poor in Southeast Asia.

Defeat in Vietnam presented the U.S. people and nation with an opportunity for repentance. Unfortunately, most churches and Christians in the United States abandoned their right to prophecy and responsible pastoral work in a post-Vietnam assessment. Their subservience to the dominant culture had sapped them of moral strength. Many had remained silent throughout the war. Other individuals and groups who had protested against U.S. policy saw Vietnam as an unusual mistake rather than as one of many foreign interventions in defense of empire. Many believed that a war that had been motivated by good intentions, such as the "defense of freedom," had gone awry.

Repentance was far from the minds of U.S. military planners and economic elites in the post-Vietnam period. They concerned themselves with developing more effective strategies of interventionism. They studied the revolutionary thoughts and experiences of Mao, Ho Chi Minh, and Che Guevara; reopened the books on previous U.S. counterinsurgency programs; and painstakingly examined the political and military strategies that had failed in Vietnam. The result of their labors is low-intensity-conflict strategy.

Lesson One: Improve Military Capacity

The highest strategic priority for the United States in the post-Vietnam era was to improve its military capacity to intervene effectively in third-world settings. I described in chapter 1, above, how low-intensity-conflict planners view the third world as the critical locus of international conflict and the front line in the defense of U.S. privilege. The development or improvement of Special Operations Forces (SOF) was a critical component in low-intensity-conflict strategy to fight effectively "World War III" or, more accurately, to wage war against the poor throughout the third world.

Lesson Two: Cost Effectiveness and Hearts and Minds

The United States failed to win in Vietnam even though it made a huge investment in dollars and U.S. lives, and despite the fact that it unleashed unprecedented firepower. This led to the conclusion that U.S. interventions need to be less costly and that the objective of warfare is not simply to win territory but to control the hearts and minds of the people. "Low intensity conflict is an economical option which we must, as a result of Vietnam, recognize as a legitimate form of conflict at least for the next twenty years," stated a former U.S. Army officer and veteran of the war in Southeast Asia. "The last quarter of the twentieth century is going to call for measured national initiatives which combine economic, psychological, and military ingredients. We cannot afford," he continued, "a military which provides only a sledgehammer in situations which demand the surgeon's scalpel."[4]

Vietnam demonstrated that the deployment of large numbers of U.S. troops and the use of unlimited firepower were expensive and not necessarily an effective means of waging war against the poor. In a similar way, military coups that changed power at the top were often incapable of controlling events and people at the base of society. Military aspects of warfare needed to be complemented by economic and psychological approaches that could influence and control hearts and minds. Properly implemented strategies of economic and psychological warfare could help drive a wedge between oppressed people and revolutionary or progressive social-change movements.

Psychological operations, according to a field manual produced by the U.S. Army, involve the "planned use of propaganda and other psychological actions to influence the opinions, emotions, attitudes, and behavior of hostile foreign groups in such a way as to support the achievement of [U.S.] national objectives."[5] A Central Intelligence Agency (CIA) manual produced for the U.S.-backed contras in Nicaragua states that once the mind of a person "has been reached, the 'political animal' has been defeated, without necessarily receiving bullets. . . . Our target, then, is the minds of the population, all the population: our troops, the enemy troops and the civilian population."[6]

Low-intensity conflict utilizes a variety of means in order to control hearts and minds and separate people from revolutionary movements. These include cosmetic economic reforms, widespread bombing, "humanitarian assistance," and terrorism. The diversity of means employed by low-intensity-conflict strategists blurs classical distinctions between military and economic aid, humanitarian assistance, and military operations. All are part of the same unified war effort.

El Salvador offers clear examples of the diversity of options used by U.S. policymakers to influence hearts and minds. The United States designed and imposed El Salvador's cosmetic land reform in an effort to draw support away from the Farabundo Martí National Liberation Front (FMLN) which had broad-based support among campesinos. However, cosmetic reforms for counterrevolutionary purposes had little success in winning hearts and minds. The United States then directed the Salvadoran military to carry out massive bombing campaigns against civilians in rural areas in an effort to displace them from their homelands, a policy similar to that employed in Vietnam. Bombing and forced displacement were followed by the delivery of "humanitarian assistance" in an effort to win support from the survivors. "Humanitarian assistance," according to a U.S. general, is "a fundamental Department of Defense mission in low intensity warfare." It is *an integral part of military operations* (italics added).[7]

There is a common saying in Central America that summarizes the fundamental contradiction in U.S. low-intensity-conflict strategy: "Everything has changed except the reality." Low-intensity conflict seeks to manage images, to control minds, and to give the appearance of reforms while leaving the structures of violence in place. It is these unjust structures (as Herbert Anaya explained in chap. 2) that victimize the poor and give rise to social rebellion. When psychological approaches and cosmetic reforms fail to pacify people and guarantee the privileges of the empire, then the appropriate measure of violence is applied through bombings or repression.

Lesson Three: Let Others Do the Dying

The challenge facing U.S. policymakers in the post-Vietnam period is to fight wars to defend perceived U.S. interests while limiting U.S. casualties. It is a conscious part of low-intensity-conflict strategy that other people do the dying in the U.S. war against the poor. Low-intensity-conflict planners cultivate and count on the conscious and unconscious racism of the U.S. people. They assume that as long as few U.S. boys return in body bags, the U.S. people will tolerate their government's questionable, illegal, even ghastly policies in third-world countries where nonwhites do the dying.

Analogies are often made between present U.S. policies in Central America and past involvement in Vietnam. These analogies are generally useful, but the U.S. experience in Vietnam led low-intensity-conflict planners to see the deployment of a significant number of U.S. fighting forces as a policy of last resort. Special Operations Forces (SOF) have been created or improved in order to lead military strikes throughout the third world, and thousands of U.S. troops have trained for a massive invasion of Central America. However, the United States prefers to wage war through less visible, covert means (including participation of some of the SOF groups) and through the use of surrogate troops like the contras and the Salvadoran military. Covert activities and the use of proxy troops are financially and politically less costly. The U.S. government avoids—for now—the public outcry that would accompany hefty tax increases and the deployment and death of thousands of U.S. soldiers. Also, by training national guard and reserve forces, the United States has adequately prepared its troops for a possible future invasion while avoiding a controversial draft that would shatter the indifference of many college students and their families.

Low-intensity conflict can be described more accurately as low-visibility warfare. The U.S. global war against the poor is being fought in the midst of shadows cast by the legacy of the "Vietnam Syndrome." Low-intensity-conflict strategy is shaped as much by the need to manage U.S. public opinion as it is by the assessment of how to fight effectively within third-world settings. Michael Klare, in *Christianity and Crisis*, writes:

> Low-intensity conflict [LIC], by definition, is that amount of murder, mutilation, torture, rape, and savagery that is sustainable without triggering widespread public disapproval at home. Or to put it another way, LIC is the ultimate in "yuppie" warfare — it allows privileged Americans to go on buying condominiums, wearing chic designer clothes, eating expensive meals at posh restaurants, and generally living in style without risking their own lives, without facing conscription, without paying higher taxes, and, most important, without being overly distracted by grisly scenes on the television set. That, essentially, is the determining characteristic of low-intensity conflict in the American context today.[8]

Lesson Four: Manage Repression and Terror

A fourth lesson that has shaped low-intensity conflict in the post-Vietnam period is the importance of making effective use of repression and terror. Low-intensity conflict is described as a strategy to counter terrorism. However, terrorism and repression are key components in its strategy of warfare against the poor. The United States terrorized civilians as part of its war effort in Vietnam. The methods of spreading terror ranged from indiscriminate bombings to targeted campaigns such as the Phoenix program through which more than 30,000 civilians thought to be sympathetic to the enemy were assassinated.

Low-intensity-conflict planners promote the use of terrorism in defense of perceived U.S. interests. Their post-Vietnam assessment was that repression and terror were essential components of U.S. warfare strategy in the third world. However, they must be managed more effectively to achieve specific goals.

The management of repression and terrorism is clearly seen in the implementation of low-intensity-conflict strategy in Central America. In El Salvador repression and terror are central to U.S. counterinsurgency efforts in defense of an unpopular government at war against its own people. Widespread bombing of civilians in the countryside served the political and military objective of displacing people from areas where the FMLN enjoyed widespread support. Human rights were also managed to respond to changing political needs and circumstances.

Herbert Anaya earlier described how the United States manipulates human rights as part of a "counterrevolutionary strategy." "Repression grows," Anaya said, "in response to the strength of popular organizations." When the popular movements were building, they were met by a period of massive repression. "After destroying the popular movements they began talking about 'respecting' human rights. The psychological terror of the people was already well established," Anaya stated. "We therefore entered a period of selective repression." As the popular movements rebounded, the groundwork was laid "to justify a new wave of repression." It was once again time "to turn the screws."

U.S. low-intensity-conflict strategy in El Salvador utilized generalized terror against civilians in order to sow fear and shape the collective memory of the people. It was hoped that once terrorized the people could be intimidated into silence with lesser amounts of violence, that is, through selective terror. If over time selective terror proved an insufficient deterrent to "the crimes of the poor," then violence escalated accordingly.

The U.S. strategy of managing terror in El Salvador can be illustrated by use of an analogy. Imagine a situation in which mass murderers kill thirty people in your politically active neighborhood for eight consecutive weeks. Among the dead are both neighborhood activists and others less active but possibly sympathetic to the ideas of such activists. Human rights groups within and outside your neighborhood protest against the violence. After eight weeks of generalized terror, daily funerals, and blood in the streets there is a significant reduction in the overt use of violence. "Only" five people are killed weekly during weeks nine and ten. All of the victims were apparently targeted for assassination because they were members of neighborhood organizations or members of local human rights groups that had demanded that the perpetrators of the violence be brought to justice.

The U.S. government cites reduced numbers of death-squad victims as "proof" of its commitment to human rights in El Salvador and the success of that commitment. The following three questions, based on the analogy above, illustrates the difference between respect for human rights and the management of terror.

1. Would a reduced body count make you and your family feel safe in your neighborhood if not one of the mass murderers had been arrested, tried before a court of law, or jailed?

2. Would a reduction in assassinations from thirty to five each week encourage you to be involved politically if you knew that while the body-count figures were down activists were being targeted for assassination and harassment?

3. What would be your response if several of your neighbors took advantage of the "safer conditions in the neighborhood" and spoke out freely, only to be killed (so that in subsequent weeks the numbers of dead averaged fifteen)?

U.S.-sponsored and -managed terrorism is not limited to counterinsurgency projects directed against the poor who are working to change U.S.-backed governments. The United States also managed the repression and terror utilized by the contras in Nicaragua as part of a *proinsurgency* campaign against a popularly elected government. Edgar Chamorro, a former high-level leader in the U.S. war against Nicaragua, left the U.S.-backed contras because he could no longer stomach the atrocities committed against civilians. Chamorro testified before the International Court of Justice (World Court) during Nicaragua's case against the United States. He indicated that terrorism was the *policy* of the U.S. government and not simply the actions of an uncontrollable surrogate force:

> A major part of my job as communications officer was to work to improve the image of the F.D.N. [the Nicaraguan Democratic Force, which is the largest contra group] forces. This was challenging, because it was standard F.D.N. practice to kill prisoners and suspected San-dinista collaborators. In talking with officers in the F.D.N. camps along the Honduran border, I frequently heard offhand remarks like, "Oh, I cut his throat." The C.I.A. did not discourage such tactics. To the contrary, the Agency severely criticized me when I admitted to the press that the F.D.N. had regularly kidnapped and executed agrarian reform workers and civilians. We were told that the only way to defeat the Sandinistas was to . . . kill, kidnap, rob and torture.[9]

If the United States is ever brought before a Nuremberg-type tribunal to assess its crimes against the poor of Central America, neither Christians living in the United States nor the nation's leaders will be able to use the argument that "we didn't know" about U.S.-sponsored terrorism. Witness for Peace and other religious groups, former CIA officials, and human rights organizations such as Americas Watch and Amnesty International have all documented and condemned U.S. support for the contras and other "friendly" governments that terrorize civilians. In what is perhaps the best human rights report on Nicaragua the London-based Catholic Institute for International Relations states that "the greatest violator of human rights in Nicaragua is neither the Sandinistas nor the contras but the U.S. government. In order to . . . re-establish unchallenged U.S. control over a region which it regards as its backyard," the report continues, "the U.S. has sac-rificed . . . Nicaraguan lives . . . and caused untold suffering."[10]

Witness for Peace has documented hundreds of cases similar to the following:

> Natividad Miranda Sosa was kidnapped and held for nine months along with her four daughters, ages 20, 15, 13 and 11. Her oldest daughter, Aureliana, was delivered to the contra leader known as "El Gato." The rest of the women were held captive by the contra leader called "El Gavilan." They were given little to eat or drink, were con-stantly guarded, and raped again and again.
>
> The 11 year old daughter, Mirian, clung to her mother until one day the contras split them up by telling Natividad she had to cook for them. Eleven year old Mirian was raped, and passed from one contra

to the next. The following night they did not touch Mirian, but for Natividad the second night was the worst. "I didn't think I would live," she related.[11]

"Encouraging techniques of raping women and executing men and children," former CIA official John Stockwell states, "is a *coordinated policy of the destabilization program*" (italics added).[12]

One other example from on-the-scene reports by Witness for Peace illustrates the human costs of U.S. support for terrorism as part of its low-intensity-conflict strategy against the poor of Nicaragua:

On a Sunday afternoon 20 men were kidnapped by the contras from the countryside surrounding Achuapa. The bodies of 13 were found in a ditch a week later. The campesinos who found the decomposing bodies, covered with rocks and logs, located them by their smell. All the remains showed signs of torture: cut out tongues, stab wounds, empty eye sockets, severed fingers and toes, castration. Most of the dead had been so badly tortured they were difficult to identify.[13]

The overall objective of U.S.-sponsored terrorism in Nicaragua was to erode popular support from a revolution whose commitment to improving the living standards of the poor was unacceptable to the empire. Generalized terror against civilians in Nicaragua, as in El Salvador, was part of a campaign to create a climate of fear and terror. The United States also encouraged the use of more selective terror in which government leaders, teachers, health workers, land-reform promoters, and others associated with the development of social programs of the government were targeted for assassination.

The CIA manual *Psychological Operations in Guerrilla Warfare*, which encouraged the contras to assassinate "government officials and sympathizers," may have been produced in order to encourage the contras to shift from the phase of warfare conducted through generalized terror into a new phase of targeted terror against civilians who were committed to the revolutionary process. "I found many of the tactics advocated in the manual to be offensive," Edgar Chamorro stated before the World Court. "I complained to the C.I.A. station chief . . . and no action was ever taken in response to my complaints. In fact,"Chamorro continued, "the practices advocated in the manual were employed by the F.D.N. troops. Many civilians were killed in cold blood. Many others were tortured, mutilated, raped, robbed or otherwise abused."[14]

Targeted repression and terror are vital components of the U.S. war against the poor. Their goal in Nicaragua was to discourage people from promoting or participating in literacy campaigns, health programs, vaccinations, forestry projects, and land reforms. The U.S.-backed contras were instructed to kill people who worked to improve the living standards of the poor in an effort to undermine the most positive gains of the Nicaraguan revolution.

Lesson Five: Redefine Victory

The central role of terrorism in low-intensity-conflict strategy against the Nicaraguan people is related to a fifth lesson learned from the U.S. war in Vietnam. The U.S. failure in Vietnam led low-intensity-conflict planners to redefine victory and defeat. The United States had "lost" the war but not entirely. Vietnam was outside U.S. control and this was an element of defeat. However, although the Vietnamese people's victory over the United States might fuel other third-world people's political struggles, the war had effectively destroyed Vietnam's economy so that it might never recover. The outcome in Vietnam, therefore, could be considered a victory for the United States because Vietnam could be pointed to as another example "of the failures of socialism."

Low-intensity-conflict planners define victory in terms of a sliding scale of acceptable outcomes. In Nicaragua, for example, there were at least three potential end-results whereby U.S. policymakers could claim victory. The first and most desirable goal was to overthrow the Nicaraguan revolution and replace it with a government subservient to U.S. interests. A replacement government would preferably have a human face and be less dictatorial than the former U.S.-backed dictatorship. However, brutality would be tolerated or encouraged if it became necessary during the course of undoing authentic reforms.

A second acceptable end-result of low-intensity-conflict strategy in Nicaragua was to make people suffer. Few U.S. policymakers believed the contras were "freedom fighters" who would overthrow an unpopular Nicaraguan government. For example, the former U.S. ambassador to Nicaragua, Anthony Quainton, openly acknowledged in meetings I attended with U.S. delegations, that the Nicaraguan revolution had widespread popular support and he rightly predicted that in fair elections the Sandinistas would win a sizable victory.

An honest assessment of the successes and deficiencies of the Nicaraguan revolution would need to consider that the purpose of proinsurgency is to shift the priorities of governments disliked by the United States from revolutionary development into warfare. Since achieving independence from the U.S.-backed dictatorship in 1979, Nicaragua has had only three years of relative peace. During those three years substantial progress was made in improving living standards. In the years that followed, despite an escalating U.S. war of aggression, Nicaragua expanded and institutionalized land and other structural economic reforms, drafted and ratified a constitution, and held internationally praised elections.

The contras within this framework of unacceptable structural reforms and improvements in living standards were not expected to win a traditional military victory. Their task was to help undermine a *popular* revolution. "It takes relatively few people and little support to disrupt the internal peace and economic stability of a small country," according to the late CIA director, William Casey. The U.S. war might not overthrow the Sandinistas, but "it will harass the government" and "waste it."[15] On another occasion Casey told the National Security Council: "We have our orders. I want the economic infrastructure hit, particularly the ports. [If the contras] can't get the job done, we'll use our own people and the Pentagon detachment. We have to get some high-visibility successes."[16] Within months the United States did use its "own people," known as Unilaterally Controlled Latino Assets, to blow up an oil pipeline at Puerto Sandino and oil storage tanks at the Nicaraguan port of Corinto. "Although the F.D.N. had nothing whatsoever to do with this operation," a former contra leader reported, "we were instructed by the CIA to publicly take responsibility in order to cover the CIA's involvement."[17]

The U.S. contra war was meant to inflict suffering and to terrorize the civilian population. The United States sought to destroy Nicaragua's economy through U.S. and contra attacks against production sites and human services and by forcing the Nicaraguan government to shift scarce resources away from development and into defense. If the people in El Salvador ever succeed in ousting the U.S.-backed government, improving living standards might still be impossible. The United States has the capacity to disrupt economic life in El Salvador through restrictions of aid and control of access to markets. The United States could also fund a contralike force that would prevent authentic development.

Suffering defined as victory helps explain the central role assigned to terrorism within the low-intensity-conflict project against Nicaragua. The Executive Summary Report of a U.S. Medical Task Force investigation of contra attacks against civilians, from January 1988, states:

> It is abhorrent that a primary goal of the contra army is the systematic destruction of the Nicaraguan rural health care system. Contra attacks are not mere accidents of war, but are part of a strategy which focuses on disrupting development work, rather than on achieving military victories. Attacks on health care are only one facet of contra strategy. Not only clinics, but schools, farms, and water projects are all targets of contra aggression. Fear of the contras is woven into the very matrix of the everyday lives of rural Nicaraguans. In the words of the November 5, 1987 report released by the respected human rights organization Americas Watch, contra violations of the laws of war are "so prevalent that these may be said to be their principal means of waging war."[18]

A third and perhaps the most ironic acceptable outcome of U.S. policy would have been a successful effort to force Nicaragua into a dependency relationship on the socialist block countries. The U.S. economic embargo against Nicaragua as well as aggressive lobbying of U.S. allies to reduce political and economic support have been regular features of U.S. policy. It may seem absurd that right-wing ideologues would work to push a nation into the clutches of the "evil empire" they despise. However, the fruit of such a distorted policy would be to confirm the worldview described in chapter 2 above, in which nonalignment is a contradiction in terms and third-world countries must choose either to accept U.S. domination or to face a U.S.-supported war.

Nicaragua, nonaligned and successfully improving the living standards of the poor within the framework of a mixed economy and political pluralism, posed a far greater threat to U.S. interests than a Soviet puppet state ever could. Pushing Nicaragua into a dependent relationship with the Soviet Union would not only have destroyed Nicaragua's indigenous model; it would have helped to justify an outright U.S. invasion of Nicaragua as well as greater interventionism throughout the third world.

Lesson Six: Deceive Your Own People

A sixth lesson learned by low-intensity-conflict planners is that the U.S. people must be targeted as part of the war to control hearts and minds. U.S. low-intensity-conflict planners fear the basic decency of the U.S. people. They engage in terrorism in defense of empire, but they know that to acknowledge openly abhorrent means and goals could undermine the national myths that hold the nation together.

I described earlier how low-intensity conflict is designed to make U.S. warfare less costly and less visible. Beyond this issue of "yuppie" warfare is the central role assigned to *disinformation* within the framework of low-intensity conflict.

Low-intensity-conflict supporters and planners believe that U.S. citizens cannot be trusted to defend the empire. "U.S. national security interests" are increasingly being defined and defended by "Oliver North-type crusaders" who operate outside the parameters of the U.S. Constitution. The weapons they use in their global war against the poor include deception and disinformation, which are targeted at the U.S. people. "Our most pressing problem is not in the Third World," a supporter of low-intensity conflict from the Rand Corporation states, "but here at home in the struggle for the minds of the people . . . . That is the most important thing there is. If we lose our own citizens, we will not have much going for us."[19]

In order not to "lose our own citizens" the U.S. government is actively engaged in campaigns of disinformation and deception. Some of these campaigns will be described more fully in the next chapter. However, several examples related to U.S. rhetoric about Nicaragua can illustrate how disinformation is used in an effort to shape public opinion in favor of the U.S. war against the poor.

The United States has consistently accused the Sandinistas of persecuting religion and of other serious violations of human rights. "The Nicaraguan people," according to President Reagan, "are trapped in a totalitarian dungeon."[20] "Some would like to ignore," he said on another occasion, "the incontrovertible evidence of the communist religious persecution — of Catholics, Jews and Fundamentalists; of their campaign of virtual genocide against the Miskito Indians."[21]

Former FDN leader Edgar Chamorro describes CIA manipulation of religion to serve political purposes both in and outside Nicaragua:

> [T]he CIA pulled a lot of "pranks" with the religious question. They paid for a book, *Christians under Fire*, written by Humberto Belli, which summarized the supposed persecution of the church in Nicaragua but had nothing to do with what was really going on inside the country. This was all part of our plan to use and take advantage of the power of the church and the beliefs of the people. We also sought to mobilize the people against the Nicaraguan government through their religious beliefs.[22]

Father Cesar Jerez, rector of the Catholic University in Nicaragua, read a letter, signed by hundreds of Nicaraguan religious leaders, at a press conference to condemn President Reagan's manipulation of religion:

> We condemn in the most forceful terms your bold proclamation of yourself as defender of faith and religion of our people. You, Mr. President, through your "brothers," the heralds of terror and death, are the one who is persecuting Christians in Nicaragua and ordering that they be kidnapped and killed.[23]

The respected human rights group Americas Watch has on numerous occasions condemned U.S. government efforts to distort the human rights record of both the Nicaraguan government and the U.S.-backed contras. Americas Watch has been critical of various aspects of the Nicaraguan government's human rights record. However, its reports confirm that, contrary to official rhetoric, Nicaragua's human rights record is far better than that of many of its neighbors. An Americas Watch Report entitled "Human Rights in Nicaragua: Reagan, Rhetoric and Reality" states:

> The Reagan Administration, since its inception, has characterized Nicaragua's revolutionary Government as a menace to the Americas and to the Nicaraguan people. Many of its arguments to this effect are derived from human rights "data," which the Administration has used in turn to justify its support for the *contra* rebels . . . . [W]e find the Administration's approach to Nicaragua deceptive and harmful.
> . . . Allegations of human rights abuse have become a major focus

of the Administration's campaign to overthrow the Nicaraguan government. Such a concerted campaign to use human rights in justifying military action is without precedent in U.S.–Latin American relations, and its effect is an unprecedented debasement of the human rights cause.[24]

The architect of disinformation in Nazi Germany was Joseph Goebbels, Hitler's minister for propaganda and national enlightenment. Goebbels managed the lies that strengthened Hitler's programs. "The important thing is to repeat [lies] . . . ," Goebbels said. "A lie, when it is repeatedly said, is transformed into the truth."[25] The Americas Watch Report describes how lies have been repeated through U.S. government information channels in an effort to discredit Nicaragua:

> . . . The misuse of human rights data has become pervasive in officials' statements to the press, in White House handouts on Nicaragua, in the annual *Country Report* on Nicaraguan human rights prepared by the State Department, and . . . in the President's own remarks.
> . . . In Nicaragua there is no systematic practice of forced disappearances, extrajudicial killings or torture — as has been the case with the "friendly" armed forces of El Salvador. . . . Nor has the Government practiced elimination of cultural or ethnic groups, as the Administration frequently claims; indeed in this respect, as in most others, Nicaragua's record is by no means so bad as that of Guatemala, whose government the Administration consistently defends. Moreover, some notable reductions in abuses have occurred in Nicaragua since 1982, despite the pressure caused by escalating external attacks.[26]

In addition to distorted images concerning the Sandinistas, low-intensity-conflict planners have repeatedly lied to cover up atrocities committed by the contras. The contra tactic of terrorizing civilians is an instrumental feature of warfare that defines suffering as victory. The evidence is compelling that U.S. officials consciously chose terrorists and terrorist tactics to carry out a war of aggression against Nicaragua:

• A secret U.S. Defense Intelligence Agency report labeled the first contra organization "a terrorist group."

• The chief of intelligence for the FDN was known to have helped plan the murder of Archbishop Oscar Romero in El Salvador in 1980.

• The contras were aided by U.S. government officials as they engaged in drug trafficking.

• In 1981 the CIA director, William Casey, arranged for Argentinian generals, experienced from a war of terror against their own people, to train the contras.

• Former contra and ex-CIA officials have publicly testified that U.S. officials encourage the use of terrorism to advance foreign-policy interests.

• The CIA manual produced for the Nicaraguan contras included instructions on "Implicit and Explicit Terror."

• Finally, according to former contra leader Edgar Chamorro, CIA trainers not only provided the contras with an instruction manual on how to utilize terrorist tactics against civilians, they also gave contra troops large knives. "A commando knife [was given], and our people, everybody wanted to have a knife like that, to kill people, to cut their throats."[27]

The United States uses public disinformation campaigns to cover up official involvement or complicity with terrorism because there is a conflict between the sensibilities of the U.S. people and utilizing terror as a basic feature of the low-intensity-conflict strategy of psychological warfare. "[T]he exposure of persistent human rights violations by the *contras* has led the Administration not to pressure *contra* leaders to enforce international codes of conduct," the Americas Watch Report cited earlier states, "but to drown U.S. public opinion with praise for the 'freedom fighters,' and to attempt to discredit all reports of their violations as inspired by communist or Sandinista propaganda."[28]

While living in Nicaragua I had the opportunity to meet with two former CIA officials, John Stockwell and David MacMichael. Each of them shared experiences that shed light on how disinformation is central to U.S. policy. In the 1970s Stockwell had managed the CIA's program to destabilize the government in Angola. MacMichael had been hired by the agency to monitor the flow of arms, which the Reagan administration said were moving with regularity and in substantial numbers between Nicaragua and El Salvador.

The arms-flow issue was extremely important because it was a major pretext used to justify U.S. support for the contras. MacMichael was granted top security clearance and he reviewed all the evidence. His contract with the CIA was not renewed when he reported that the massive arms flow from Nicaragua to the FMLN in El Salvador was an invention of the Reagan administration.

Stockwell described how in Angola he and other CIA officials regularly produced articles for overseas wire services that severely distorted reality but served to promote illegal U.S. policy goals. He also indicated that there are "many" U.S. journalists writing for major U.S. newspapers who are employees of the Central Intelligence Agency. Disinformation, according to Stockwell, is more important than ever because the United States is now implementing low-intensity-conflict strategy on a global basis and is actively working to destabilize one-third of the world's underdeveloped countries.

Stockwell and MacMichael had experienced the CIA from different places. Stockwell worked as a high-level agent deeply involved in covert activities that he now believes had been both illegal and immoral. MacMichael worked as a high-level CIA analyst managing information used to justify such activities. Both came to the same conclusion based on their insider's view of the Central Intelligence Agency: the fundamental purpose of the CIA is not information gathering, as most citizens believe; it is *to carry out disinformation campaigns in service to illegal presidential objectives*.

U.S.-STYLE TOTALITARIANISM

Low-intensity conflict integrates economic, psychological, diplomatic, and military aspects of warfare into a comprehensive strategy to protect "U.S. valuables" against the needs and demands of the poor. It is a total-itarianlike system designed to control the hearts and minds, the economic life, and the political destiny of people. It uses terror and repression to intimidate or punish, cosmetic reforms to pacify or disguise real intent, and disinformation to cover its bloody tracks. It defines the poor as enemy, consciously employs other peoples to die while defending "U.S. interests," and makes use of flexible military tactics.

The diversity of weapons within the low-intensity-conflict arsenal is what makes the U.S. war against the poor so insidious and destructive. The United States cannot control all events. It can, however, block meaningful social change and punish "enemies" by integrating economic, psychological, dip-lomatic, and military aspects of warfare into a comprehensive strategy that includes suffering in its definition of victory. Each of these aspects of war-fare, which have been used in the U.S. war against the people of Nicaragua, are described briefly below.

Economic Warfare

Economic warfare against the people of Nicaragua has taken a variety of forms.

• A U.S. aid package to Nicaragua approved by the U.S. Congress in 1980, a year after the ouster of the U.S.-backed dictatorship, targeted the most reactionary business organization for substantial aid. The hope was to strengthen conservative groups in Nicaragua who would work to block any major restructuring of the society on behalf of the poor. The aid package specifically prevented U.S. money from being used for education or health programs in which Cubans might be involved.

• As the revolution began to deepen reforms, the United States cut off previously approved aid. It also transferred Nicaragua's sugar quota to other "friendly" Central American countries so that Nicaragua was no longer able to sell a specified volume of sugar in the U.S. market at above world-market prices.

• In the first few years following the successful ouster of the dictatorship, Nicaragua's primary source of development capital was from multilateral lending institutions such as the World Bank. The United States has voting power in the World Bank proportional to its donations to the bank and was successful in its lobbying effort to cut off loans to Nicaragua. John Booth, in a book on the Nicaraguan revolution, provides this summary of Nicaragua's relationship to the U.S.-dominated World Bank:

> The advent of the Reagan administration . . . led to a suspension of U.S. assistance to Nicaragua and to concerted U.S. pressure on multilateral lenders to curtail loans. . . . Multilateral assistance to Nicaragua in 1979–1980 had made up 48 percent of the country's new aid commitments, but under U.S. pressure multinational lenders cut back sharply so that for 1981–1983 they provided just below 15 percent of Nicaragua's aid. As an example of the new, hard-nosed policy of the multinational lenders, the World Bank's case stands out: It had lent the Somoza regime $56 million during the final stages of the 1979 war yet forced the Sandinista government to *repay* a total of $29 million between 1980 and 1982.

Booth goes on to describe how U.S. economic and military harassment put financial pressures on Nicaragua, curtailed development, and opened up the possibility of greater dependence on the socialist bloc:

> . . . Nicaragua's early progress in curbing imports, raising grain production, and other reform and austerity measures were undermined badly by new needs for foreign borrowing imposed by the burgeoning defense burden . . . . Foreign borrowing continued at a high rate, and as the United States succeeded in shutting down its own and multilateral credits, Nicaragua turned to new lenders in the socialist bloc and to European and Latin Americans for more aid than they had given in the past. Although the United States had failed to isolate Nicaragua from Western assistance, the war and the credit crunch had both damaged Nicaragua's financial independence and converted the country into an important new client for socialist lenders.[29]

• On May 1, 1985, President Reagan declared an embargo as part of the U.S. economic war to impose suffering on the Nicaraguan people. By law an economic embargo can be issued only by presidential decree if the national security of the United States is imminently threatened. Therefore, "in response to the emergency situation created by the Nicaraguan Government's aggressive activities in Central America," President Reagan said:

> I, Ronald Reagan, President of the United States of America, find that the policies and actions of the Government of Nicaragua constitute an unusual and extraordinary threat to the national security and foreign policy of the United States and hereby declare a national emergency to deal with that threat.

Unknown to most U.S. citizens, we have been living under a state of *national emergency* in order to justify an embargo against a nation of 3 million people, three-fourths of whom are women or children under the age of fifteen.

• The United States has restricted shipments of humanitarian aid to Nicaragua from organizations such as Oxfam America.

• The United States has used debt as a weapon against its allies in Central America in order to force them to cooperate with U.S. efforts to destroy Nicaragua. The ability to exploit indebtedness is a powerful weapon in the U.S. economic-warfare arsenal. Honduras is commonly referred to in Central America as "the U.S.S. Honduras." It was transformed into a virtual military base for the United States and a staging area for the U.S.-backed contras. Honduran subservience to U.S. interests is captured in a one-line joke, which states that "Honduras is a country which needs to nationalize its own government." Dependency, which accompanies indebtedness, becomes an embarrassing affront to national sovereignty and occasionally gives rise to anti-U.S. protests. A massive debt leaves Honduras few political alternatives to U.S. domination.

El Salvador and Costa Rica share a similar fate. Neither could function without daily infusions of U.S. aid. The president of Costa Rica in 1987 launched the "Arias Peace Plan" in an effort to find a peaceful resolution to the problems in Central America. The Nobel Peace Prize committee expressed its approval of Arias's peacemaking efforts by granting him its highest honor. At the same time, the United States expressed its disapproval through economic pressure. U.S. journalists Martha Honey and Tony Avirgan, stationed in Costa Rica, reported:

> Since Arias first proposed his Central American Peace Plan in February, the Reagan administration has used a number of political and economic tactics to express its displeasure. . . . These tactics include the nondisbursement for the last six months of U.S. economic assistance to Costa Rica, the failure to appoint a new U.S. ambassador, a campaign to force the resignation of a liberal Arias advisor, maneuvers to block international bank loans to Costa Rica and restrictions on Costa Rican exports to the U.S.[30]

• Finally, as previously discussed, "military pressure" from the contras was the principal means by which the United States waged economic war against the people of Nicaragua. The contras destroyed the economic infrastructure of the country and assassinated social-development workers. The U.S.-sponsored contra war also forced the Nicaraguan government to shift resources from development into defense.

Psychological Warfare

U.S. psychological-warfare operations in Central America included elements such as the following:

• The United States sponsors radio stations that beam anti-Sandinista, pro-contra propaganda into Nicaragua. U.S. propaganda reaches all parts of Nicaragua from stations in Costa Rica, Honduras, and El Salvador. A typical message I heard while listening to radio broadcasts in northern Nicaragua accused the Sandinistas of "burning churches, kidnapping Nicaraguan children and sending them to Cuba, stealing land from campesinos, creating internal food shortages by sending Nicaragua's food to the Soviet Union, and killing old people in order to make soap."

• The United States manages the news in other Central American countries in order to portray Nicaragua as a threat to its neighbors. Nicaragua was portrayed to its neighbors as a dangerous enemy in order to take attention away from internal injustices that could fuel social tensions within other Central American countries. A Honduran priest who visited Nicaragua said that if campesinos in Honduras knew about Nicaragua's land reform, there would be a revolution in Honduras. Edgar Chamorro, recruited by the CIA to manage communications for the contras, testified before the World Court:

> The C.I.A. station in Tegucigalpa, which at the time included about 20 agents working directly with the F.D.N., gave me money, in cash, to hire several writers, reporters, and technicians to prepare a monthly bulletin . . . , to run a clandestine radio station, and to write press releases. . . . I was also given money by the C.I.A. to bribe Honduran journalists and broadcasters to write and speak favorably about the F.D.N. and to attack the Government of Nicaragua and call for its overthrow. Approximately 15 Honduran journalists and broadcasters were on the C.I.A.'s payroll, and our influence was thereby extended to every major Honduran newspaper and radio and television station. I learned from my C.I.A. colleagues that the same tactic was employed in Costa Rica in an effort to turn the newspapers and radio and television stations of that country against the Nicaraguan Government.[31]

• The use of deception and disinformation as discussed earlier is a central feature in low-intensity conflict's psychological-war techniques. The war of images includes circulation of lies through the Central Intelligence Agency, the State Department, and presidential and cabinet-officer speeches. The degree to which the U.S. press has become complicit in this deadly war of images is revealed by how frequently articles or news reports in the mainstream television and print media describe Nicaragua by using adjectives such as "Marxist," "Cuban-backed," "Marxist-Leninist," "leftist," "Soviet-backed," and "totalitarian." "Inflammatory terms, loosely used," an Americas Watch Report states, "are of particular concern. . . . Such epithets seek to prejudice public debate through distortion."[32]

• The U.S. strategy of keeping its war against the poor invisible to the

U.S. people is an important aspect in the psychological war. Low-intensity conflict's use of surrogate troops, for example, is designed to keep us from having to confront the psychological trauma of the pain and death we sponsor. In a similar way, U.S. national guard and reserve forces participate in "civic-action" projects in Central America designed to promote positive psychological images of U.S. involvement in the region. U.S. forces, like wolves in sheep's clothing, pull teeth and build roads during training exercises that equip repressive indigenous troops while providing U.S. soldiers with experience that would be vital during a future U.S. invasion of Central America.

• The United States has conducted ongoing military maneuvers and training exercises in Central America as part of its psychological war of intimidation against the Nicaraguan people. "Military deception is an aspect of strategy and tactics that is often used but seldom acknowledged . . . ," the U.S. Army field manual, *Psychological Operations, Techniques and Procedures*, states. "Deception is the deliberate misrepresentation of reality done to gain a competitive advantage."[33]

On July 19, 1983 on the fourth anniversary of the Nicaraguan revolution, the Pentagon sent nineteen warships with 16,000 U.S. marines to Nicaragua's coasts. On another occasion the United States surrounded the tiny country of Nicaragua with (a) twenty-five warships off both coasts, carrying nearly 25,000 soldiers and 150 fighter bombers, and (b) an additional 20,000 U.S., Honduran, and contra troops that were moved to Nicaragua's northern border. "The firepower on the three armadas exceeded any maritime deployment during the entire course of the Vietnam war."[34] Anyone who has visited Nicaragua has witnessed the emotional toll that U.S. psychological-warfare operations, including ongoing training exercises and threats of invasion, have had on the Nicaraguan people.

• The most widely used psychological tool in the low-intensity-conflict arsenal is terrorism. In the case of Nicaragua, U.S.-managed terrorism was meant to punish a nation that had freed itself from the empire and had begun improving the living standards of its people.

U.S. low-intensity-conflict strategy utilized generalized and targeted terrorism in Nicaragua in service to a broader geopolitical, psychological objective. Terrorism was part of the U.S. war against hope. The U.S. war to destroy revolutionary gains in education and health care and to reduce living standards in Nicaragua was part of a broader psychological war to discourage other third-world peoples from challenging U.S. power. Nicaragua was, and as of this writing continues to be, a ray of hope for oppressed people in Central America and throughout the world. The U.S. low-intensity-conflict strategy of terror, death, and destruction is meant to demonstrate to third-world peoples the high costs of embarking upon a road to self-determination.

Diplomatic Warfare

U.S. diplomatic-warfare efforts have included the following elements:
• The United States actively worked to discredit Nicaragua's elections.

Leaders from various opposition political parties told me that the U.S. embassy offered them bribes in an effort to get them to withdraw from Nicaragua's electoral process in 1984. While pointing out some deficiencies in Nicaragua's electorial process, Americas Watch reported that "the Sandinista Party achieved a popular mandate, while the opposition parties that chose to participate secured some 30 percent of the seats in the Constituent Assembly."[35]

Auturo Cruz, a candidate whose absence from the elections was most often cited by U.S. officials as evidence of "sham" elections, has admitted to accepting CIA money in order not to run. Just prior to Nicaragua's elections and before Cruz's relationship with the CIA became public, the highly respected Western European leader, Willy Brandt, stated:

> One must not make the mistake of thinking that Cruz's group is the only opposition group that exists in Nicaragua . . . . It is astonishing that [U.S. Secretary of State] Shultz is calling the Nicaraguan elections a sham because a sector of the opposition decided not to run of its own accord.[36]

U.S. diplomatic and psychological warfare techniques converged during efforts to discredit Nicaragua's elections. In an effort to take U.S. and world attention away from the positive assessments of Nicaragua's electoral process, the U.S. manufactured a "MIG" crisis. Nicaragua, according to disinformation sources from the United States, was about to receive advanced fighter jets from the Soviet Union. The U.S. media focused attention on the crisis for days. Democrats and Republicans in Congress tripped over themselves as they competed to see who could better justify direct U.S. military action when the MIG jets arrived. The United States canceled leave for army troops at Fort Bragg and mobilized thousands of others for land, sea, and air maneuvers off the coast of Nicaragua. As it turned out, the ship's cargo did not contain MIG jets but it did include donations of toys for the upcoming Christmas.

● The United States as part of its diplomatic war effort also worked to narrow Nicaragua's options in terms of aid, trade, and military assistance. The United States succeeded in cutting off multilateral aid, aggressively lobbied allies to reduce economic assistance, and slapped a trade embargo on Nicaragua. It also refused Nicaragua's early request for help in developing its armed forces and punished France for agreeing to a military assistance program. This left Nicaragua with few options for military supplies apart from reliance upon the Soviet Union, a dependency that deepened as the U.S. war against Nicaragua escalated.

● The United States actively worked to undermine regional peace initiatives. Economic and diplomatic pressures were used to confront the "menace of peace." The Arias Peace Plan and the Contadora Peace Process were considered dangerous for several reasons. First, the involvement of Latin American nations in regional peace efforts was seen as a dangerous precedent that ultimately threatened the Monroe Doctrine. In the eyes of low-intensity-conflict planners, regional initiatives were signs of a deeper and potentially far more dangerous rebellion challenging Latin America's "backyard status" within the U.S. empire. The Arias and Contadora peace initiatives would have curtailed U.S. "rights" to use military force in the region. Equally important, a peacemaking role for Latin American nations encouraged regional discussions of pressing economic problems, including alternatives to paying Latin America's crippling debt. Undermining regional peace plans, therefore, was part of a broader power struggle in which the United States sought to reassert its authority over Latin America.

Second, both the Arias and the Contadora peace initiatives were resisted because they acknowledged the legitimacy of the Nicaraguan government while delegitimizing U.S. policies. Peace was a terrifying prospect for low-intensity-conflict planners who understood that their mission was to overthrow, punish, or destroy the Nicaraguan revolution. Their crusade against social improvements and hope as part of a global offensive against the poor was incompatible with regional peace.

• The United States engaged in international slander campaigns against the Nicaraguan government similar to those used to deceive its own people. It also managed terrorism in El Salvador in which high body counts were discouraged in favor of selective applications of terror. This was part of its diplomatic initiative to quiet critics in and outside the United States.

• Finally, the most sophisticated weapon in the U.S. diplomatic arsenal was the use of elections for undemocratic purposes. Low-intensity conflict uses elections to create an image of democracy while continuing to assign real power to U.S. officials and military and economic elites. (The dangers of seriously distorting democracy at home and abroad will be discussed in more detail in chap. 4, below.)

Low-Intensity Conflict and Its Military Aspects

Among the military aspects of low-intensity conflict are the following.

• The United States has expanded and improved Special Operations Forces to intervene more effectively in third-world settings.

• Low-intensity conflict relies heavily on U.S. training, supply, and management of surrogate forces such as the Nicaraguan contras and the military forces of "friendly" countries.

• Military activities against Nicaragua have included covert operations carried out through groups such as the National Security Council, the CIA, and other "secret teams" of mercenaries, arms merchants, and drug-runners.

• U.S. military maneuvers and training exercises prepare U.S. troops for possible future invasions while serving as present instruments of psychological warfare.

• U.S. planes have regularly violated international law by entering Nicaragua's air space to provide the contras with logistical support in their war against the Nicaraguan people.

• Finally, the United States has relied upon third-country suppliers such as Israel, Saudi Arabia, and South Korea to provide valuable military support for the contras during periods when the U.S. Congress restricted open U.S. aid.

CONCLUSION

The United States is a conservative superpower facing many challenges in a world of rapid economic and social change. Low-intensity conflict, for now and for the foreseeable future, is assigned the task of defending and expanding U.S. power and privilege throughout the third world. Low-intensity-conflict strategy is part of a U.S. global war against the poor designed to manage social change in ways that protect perceived U.S. interests while maintaining, at least for its own people, the image of democratic ideals.

I am often asked questions about differences between Democrats and Republicans with regard to U.S. policy in Central America. Low-intensity conflict is a bipartisan effort to defend U.S. privileges. While Democrats and Republicans have tactical differences over how best to intervene in defense of U.S. interests they share fundamental values and concerns. In recent years, Democrats more than Republicans have seemed troubled by overt use of terrorism. Some may be reluctant to embrace terrorism because it offends their moral sensibilities. Other doubt its expendiency.

It is likely that low-intensity-conflict planners, in the post-Reagan phase of their global war against the poor, will continue creatively to mix military, economic, psychological and diplomatic aspects of warfare in response to specific needs. In El Salvador we are likely to witness an escalation of overt violence. In Nicaragua the U.S.-sponsored war and natural disaster (Hurricane Joan devastated the country in October, 1988) have combined to undermine the gains of the Nicaraguan revolution. This could lead the United States to place less emphasis on military pressure through the contras and greater emphasis on economic and diplomatic pressures. U.S. policy makers may conclude that suffering in Nicaragua is now sufficient to dim the light of the Nicaraguan revolution in the eyes of poor people throughout the world. This could encourage a policy that would involve some form of public accommodation with the Sandinistas coupled with non-military forms of harassment.

Questions about differences between Republicans and Democrats ignore more fundamental issues. A more urgent question is this: Will U.S. citizens recognize in time to save themselves and others that low-intensity-conflict strategy is far more compatible with fascism than democracy?

4

Distorted Democracy

My objective all along was to withhold from the Congress exactly what the [National Security Council] was doing in carrying out the President's policy [toward Nicaragua].

John Poindexter, former National Security Advisor

... destroy this letter after reading.... We need to make sure that this new financing [for the contras] does *not* become known. The Congress must believe that there continues to be an urgent need for funding.

Lt. Col. Oliver North[1]

Iran/Contragate did not begin with Oliver North. Nor is the scandal just about Iran and Nicaragua. For a quarter century, a Secret Team of U.S. military and CIA officials, acting both officially and on their own, have waged secret wars, toppled governments, trafficked in drugs, assassinated political enemies, stolen from the U.S. government, and subverted the will of the Constitution, the Congress, and the American people.

The Christic Institute

INTRODUCTION

Miguel D'Escoto, Catholic priest and head of the Nicaraguan Foreign Ministry, looked tired as he sat down to address a delegation of foreign visitors. D'Escoto had recently completed a fifteen-day march for peace from the Honduran border to Managua. It had been a march "to touch the heart of God," he said, and to call people of faith in his own country and throughout the world to bolder action to stop the U.S. war against Nicaragua.

D'Escoto agreed to answer questions. "Why did the United States break off bilateral talks with Nicaragua?" "What is the present status of the

Contadora Peace Process?" "Why do you periodically take a leave of absence from official government duties in order to fast, pray, and march for peace?" "Do you really think prayers and fasts and blisters on your feet will change U.S. policies?"

D'Escoto responded to these and other concerns for about ninety minutes. There was time for one last question. U.S. delegations visiting Central America have oftentimes learned that an open-ended final question is a good way to end a session. "What message would you like us to take back to the U.S. people?" someone asked. "Tell them," D'Escoto said, "that *we* are deeply concerned about *them.*"

The group, myself included, was somewhat taken aback by D'Escoto's response. Most of us were expecting to hear challenging words about our responsibility to end a brutal war, financed with our tax dollars, that was imposing suffering on the Nicaraguan people. "Tell them," he continued, "that we are deeply concerned about them because a country that exports repression will one day unleash that repression against its own people. A nation that wages war against the poor in Nicaragua will ignore the needs of its own poor. A country which in the name of 'democracy' fights wars against the self-determination of other peoples cannot remain a democracy. I have felt for a long time," he concluded, "that the U.S. people will one day be the most repressed people in the world."

U.S. citizens remain largely indifferent to the suffering of others caused by low-intensity conflict and the U.S. war against the poor. Many of us have been pacified through the sweet-sounding rhetoric about "freedom and democracy." However, the abuse of democracy is a long-standing component of U.S. foreign policy and a central aspect of low-intensity-conflict strategy. If we are not more vigilant in defending authentic democracy, then the tyranny that the United States has exported for so long may finally come home to roost.

DEMOCRACY AND THE FIFTH FREEDOM

No nation on earth has a stronger verbal commitment to freedom and to democratic principles than the United States. However, this verbal commitment bears little or no resemblance to the historical record of U.S. interventionism in defense of privilege. Rhetoric about freedom and democracy has served as a convenient cover for the defense of the freedom to rob and exploit.

The "myth of democratic ideals" has managed to survive despite near constant military and economic interventions in defense of dictatorships or unrepresentative governments throughout the globe. U.S. support for dictators in Cuba, Iran, the Philippines, Nicaragua, Brazil, South Korea, Argentina, and numerous other places did not prevent our leaders from talking with a straight face about "freedom and democracy." Dozens of U.S. military interventions in Central America, invasions of the Dominican Republic and

Grenada, a several-decade-long war in Vietnam, covert activities that ousted democratically elected governments in Guatemala and Chile, economic backing for the racist regime in South Africa, and World Court decisions condemning U.S. policies in Central America have not dampened our capacity for self-serving myths.

Behind the myths lies a historical record demonstrating that the economic demands of empire lead to a curious definition of freedom. The president of Business International, Orville Freeman, describes the period following World War II, a period in which the United States solidified its relationships with dictatorships in Latin America and throughout much of the world, as an exemplary time of freedom. "Following World War II the U.S. followed a very enlightened policy of free trade and free investment," Freeman said. "... [It was] a very open world, and a very stable world. So this was one of the periods of freedom: freedom to invest, freedom to trade, freedom to have economic intercourse. Stability and freedom."[2]

U.S. foreign policy has rarely if ever concerned itself with promoting democracy. It has been assigned the difficult task of providing a stable climate for U.S. economic expansion and investment in a world of stark inequalities. The treasurer of Standard Oil of New Jersey stated in 1946:

> American private enterprise is confronted with this choice; it may strike out and save its position all over the world, or sit by and witness its own funeral. . . . We must set the pace and assume the responsibility of the majority stockholder in this corporation known as the world. . . . This is a permanent obligation. . . . Our foreign policy will be more concerned with the safety and stability of our foreign investments than ever before.[3]

Poor people throughout the world own little or no stock in this corporate world. They are disenfranchised politically and economically. Their hope of improving living standards depends on political and economic reforms that are essential for economic development and authentic democracy. Frances Moore Lappe and Joseph Collins, in discussing the "causes of powerlessness," note that "the root cause of hunger isn't scarcity of food or land; *it's a scarcity of democracy.*" They go on to say:

> Democratic structures are those in which people have a say in decisions that most affect their well-being. Leadership can be kept accountable to the needs of the majority. Antidemocratic structures are those in which power is so tightly concentrated that the majority of people are left with no say at all. Leaders are accountable only to the powerful minority. . . .
>
> As long as this fundamental concept of democracy—accountability to those most affected by decisions—is absent from economic life, people will continue to be made powerless . . . . Poverty and hunger

will go on destroying the lives of millions each year and scarring the lives of hundreds of millions more.[4]

According to Lappe and Collins there is a need for greater democracy at the level of the family, the village, the nation, and the international economy.

Hunger and poverty are consequences of a lack of democracy. The poor would not choose to starve if they had the freedom to participate democratically in economic as well as political life. The stark inequalities that exist within and between nations cry out for the need to redistribute power and to increase the capacity of people to participate in meaningful ways in decisions that affect their lives. U.S. foreign policy sets out to restrict this freedom in defense of the rights of powerful minorities, who exercise their freedom and power to exploit the resources and markets of impoverished nations. In 1975 an executive of Best Foods noted that future markets in Latin America looked good for U.S. corporations "with a continental vision," although the markets would be limited to select groups. Of Latin America's total population,

a fifth will be able to buy, through their economic power, almost all the products which the industrialists here presently manufacture, while a third will be able to buy some of these products only very infrequently. The rest of the population, about half of the total, are not customers except for the most simple and basic products and probably will continue on a subsistence basis.[5]

The U.S. war against the poor is a war against the democratic aspirations of the majority of the human family. There is a fundamental contradiction between authentic democracy and empire, the well-being of the poor and minority alliances between elites. Freedom defined as the free movement of capital and free trade has rewarded elites while leaving the poor free to be hungry, landless, sick and persecuted. In chapter 2 I described how, from the perspective of U.S. policy makers, Nicaragua's "greatest crime" was to "redistribute wealth from the rich to the poor." There is a parallel "crime" in the context of this discussion about democracy: Nicaragua is dangerous and must be destroyed, according to low-intensity-conflict planners, because *it is one of the few countries in the world where economic privilege does not guarantee political control.*

Democracy, consistent with prevailing myths, is a fundamental concern for U.S. leaders. Ironically, however, this concern is most acute whenever people exercise their democratic rights to challenge unjust applications of U.S. power. For example, business leaders in the aftermath of the popular protests that challenged U.S. involvement in Vietnam complained about too much democracy in the United States.[6] In a similar way, free elections are held up by U.S. leaders as essential for democracy unless political parties opposed to U.S. interests win. The U.S. war against the poor has meant an effort to invalidate, destabilize, or destroy democracies that have included or encouraged significant participation from or power for the poor.

Democratically elected governments in Guatemala, Chile, and Jamaica were overthrown or destabilized through a combination of U.S. covert and overt pressures. In Guatemala and Chile, the United States strengthened right-wing elements within the military in order to overthrow democratic systems and replace them with military dictators. In Jamaica and Chile conservative business leaders and international bankers worked to make the economy scream. In Nicaragua the contras have been hired to terrorize civilians, cripple the economy, and erode the political and economic gains of the poor.

The U.S. practice of making democracy compatible with dictatorship, poverty, and repression led respected Latin American leader, Carlos Andres Perez to say:

> What North Americans don't understand is that in the long run we share a common fate—a past and a present that implicate North America in the skewed development and upheavals of the rest of the hemisphere. For decades, the United States baffled us with its un-conditional support for Central American dictators—so much so that many Latin Americans now suspect the word "democracy." The dic-tators created exclusive societies based on systematic injustice—breed-ing grounds for explosive discontent. . . .
>
> Can't the United States see that conflict is inevitable in countries besieged by poverty and political subjugation? . . .
>
> Our problems smolder, then burst into flame, but one thing remains constant: the unbearable paternalism of the United States and its apparent distrust of any Latin American with a sense of self-respect.

ELECTIONS WITHIN LOW-INTENSITY-CONFLICT STRATEGY

A common feature of U.S. foreign policy for more than a century has been the use of elections for undemocratic purposes. Elections in the age of low-intensity conflict are generally managed more efficiently than in the past when ballot boxes were stuffed and opposition candidates killed, bribed, or exiled. Elections are an important part of the U.S. diplomatic war effort and they make valuable contributions to wars that are fought with both images and bullets. In fact elections are often carried out so that bullets and bombs can continue arriving in record numbers. The militaries in Honduras, El Salvador, and Guatemala (the real power brokers along with the U.S. embassy and economic elites) agreed to U.S. plans for elections in the 1980s after the United States assured them that, following the elections, their power would be enhanced through large increases in military assistance.

In El Salvador in the early 1980s, the myth of U.S. commitments to democracy was being buried along with murdered nuns, an assassinated archbishop, and thousands of tortured civilians. Elections were carried out as part of the same strategy that brought about the shift from generalized to selective terror. In the pre-low-intensity-conflict stage of counterinsurgency, the U.S. openly backed repressive dictators in order to "protect national valuables" and to defend U.S. interests against "the crimes of the poor."

Low-intensity-conflict strategists recognize that dictators sometimes outlive their usefulness. Dictators become liabilities when they can no longer effectively serve as guardians of U.S. interests, that is, at the point when their repression and corruption give rise to social turmoil beyond their control. For example, the Reagan administration and the mainstream press heaped praise on the Marcos dictatorship in the Philippines for its commitments to "democracy" until Marcos could no longer control the people or protect U.S. investments. When Marcos himself became a source of instability he was no longer "democratic" and he was gone.

Elections are essential when authoritarian governments fail, although the opposite is also true. Elections are part of low-intensity conflict's preferred strategy to protect U.S. interests in the third world. However, preferences will nearly always give way to a pragmatic course of action if circumstances dictate a lifting of the democratic façade. Within low-intensity-conflict strategy *elections are not a means of establishing a basis of real power*, although elections may be part of a broader plan to reshuffle power among elites. *They are a means of masking power.*

Elections in El Salvador, like those held elsewhere as part of low-intensity-conflict strategy, did not change the fundamental power relationships within the country. The hierarchy of power remained the U.S. embassy at the pinnacle, the Salvadoran military and economic elites a little below, and the civilian government looking good in U.S. papers but nearly powerless in practice. U.S.-sponsored elections, like cosmetic land reform and managed terror, were part of the "war of images." They were necessary ingredients in a diplomatic offensive to counter congressional opposition and unfavorable domestic and international public opinion.

In April 1988 I visited with a priest in El Salvador who, for reasons of safety, prefers not to be publicly identified. "El Salvador," he said, "is like a big farm and the house that directs the farm is the U.S. embassy." The quotation in context reads:

> The U.S. is not interested in creating democracy in El Salvador. They are interested in their own project to keep control. They needed the Christian Democrats in order to carry out this project, although they will also work with ARENA [a right-wing party with close ties to the death squads]. The U.S. war project in El Salvador is designed to maintain a situation here like they have in Honduras where the U.S.

decides what the people can and must do. El Salvador is like a big farm and the house that directs the farm is the U.S. embassy.

The U.S. project is not democracy. The U.S. project is to use "democracy" to muffle international criticism in order better to control El Salvador. "Democracy" is a façade to cover many unpleasant things.

COVERT OPERATIONS: ERODING DEMOCRACY WITHIN

Using elections for undemocratic purposes is only one example of United States manipulation of democracy in its war against the poor. There is another serious attack against democracy that is central to low-intensity-conflict strategy: a reliance upon secrecy and illegal covert operations.

Low-intensity conflict, as stated earlier, is meant to make the U.S. war against the poor less visible, less costly, and less offensive to the U.S. people. Secrecy and covert operations are well suited to a deceptive war of images that is designed to hide real policy goals and the means that are utilized to achieve them. They have been responsible for widespread human suffering around the world while at the same time they have come to pose a serious threat to democracy in the United States.

The United States took a significant step toward becoming a national security state with the passage of the National Security Act of 1947. This act created the Central Intelligence Agency and the National Security Council. The ethical grounding for these agencies was the belief that the United States could and should use *any means* in order to defend its interests. A secret report prepared for the White House in 1954 by a group of prominent citizens, including former President Herbert Hoover, states:

> It is now clear that we are facing an implacable enemy whose avowed objective is world domination. . . . There are no rules in such a game. Hitherto accepted norms of human conduct do not apply. . . . If the United States is to survive, long-standing American concepts of fair play must be reconsidered. . . . We must learn to subvert, sabotage and destroy our enemies by more clever, sophisticated, more effective methods than those used against us.[7]

The Central Intelligence Agency and its significant network of contacts and agents became a sort of "presidential hit squad" that, in the name of "national security," was sent out to "subvert, sabotage and destroy our enemies." The means used to carry out covert operations not only violated "hitherto accepted norms of human conduct," they oftentimes circumvented the law, the will of Congress, and the consciences and political wishes of the U.S. public. "What you have," says Morton Halperin, who directs the Washington office of the American Civil Liberties Union, "is a growing gap between the perceptions inside the executive branch about what the threats are to our national security, and the beliefs in the Congress and the public about the threats to national security." Halperin once resigned his staff position on the National Security Council in protest over U.S. policy in Vietnam and Cambodia. He continues:

[The gap in perceptions about the meaning of national security] leads to secrecy; that is what drives the policy underground, that's what leads the president to rely more on covert operations, what leads the president and his officials to lie to the public, then lie to the Congress about the operation. Precisely because they cannot get their way in public debate, they are driven to seek to circumvent the democratic process.[8]

An affidavit submitted to the U.S. federal court by Daniel Sheehan of the Christic Institute describes the tragic results of circumventing the democratic process. The Christic Institute lawsuit charged a group of defendants, many of whom were key players in the Iran-contra scandal, with participation in a criminal conspiracy. ". . . These defendants, some of whom have been tagged by the press as 'contrapreneurs,' represent the very epitome of organized crime, but on an international stage. They deal wholesale in narcotic drugs, illegal weapons and violence," the affidavit charges. "Rather than take over local businesses or undermine local government, they seek to take over whole nations. They do not hesitate to murder and destroy anyone or anything that gets in their way."[9]

A brief summary of the Christic Institute's affidavit illustrates how covert activities, so central to low-intensity-conflict strategy, are incompatible with democracy. According to the Christic Institute lawsuit:

• Behind the Iran-contra scandal there is a "secret team," operating inside and outside the U.S. government, which has over a period of more than twenty-five years powerfully influenced or controlled U.S. foreign policy.

• Members of the secret team constituted "a virtual shadow government, directed by unelected officials of the National Security Council and the Central Intelligence Agency, and a private network of former military and intelligence officials. In conducting unauthorized covert operations, members of the secret network placed themselves above the law in the name of 'national security.' "[10]

• Members of the shadow government were deeply involved in assassinations, drug- and gun-running activities, and covert actions. Consistent with the Hoover Report's recommendations that the United States had to reconsider "long-standing American concepts of fair play" and "learn to subvert, sabotage and destroy our enemies," the shadow government built alliances between U.S. government officials, the Mafia, and international drug cartels; assassinated many thousands of civilians in Southeast Asia; carried out or attempted assassination of foreign leaders; trained death squads and secret police forces; worked to shore up unpopular dictators like the Shah of Iran and the Somoza dictatorship in prerevolutionary Nicaragua; worked to destabilize "unfriendly" governments such as Allende in Chile and the Sandinistas in Nicaragua; cooperated with the Colombian drug cartel to plot the assassination of the former U.S. ambassador to Costa Rica, Lewis Tambs, with the intention of justifying a U.S. invasion of Nicaragua by blaming his death on the Sandinistas; contracted with the Reagan administration and the National Security Council to find ways of circumventing a congressional ban prohibiting aid to the contras, including the trading of arms to Iran in exchange for hostages and money for the contras; illegally shipped weapons from the United States to the contras and allowed returning planes to use the same protected flight paths to transport drugs into the United States;[11] targeted the U.S. people for disinformation campaigns; and helped prepare contingency plans for declaring a form of martial law in the United States that would have formally suspended constitutional freedoms.

• The existence of a shadow government of unelected officials, acting independently or at times in cooperation with elected officials, presents the United States with a serious constitutional crisis:

> This shadow government, sanctioned and shielded by the Reagan Administration, has violated the separation of powers doctrine that is the bedrock of our constitutional system. The contra supply operation circumvented and denied Congress its two most important constitutional powers: the authority to declare war and the power to withhold or appropriate funds.
>
> The secrecy and deception required by covert operations are incompatible with our democracy. Abroad, these operations violate international law and our obligation to respect the sovereignty and self-determination of other nations. The survival of our constitutional system requires the restoration of public accountability and openness, the rule of law, and a responsible foreign policy.[12]

Whether or not the Christic Institute succeeds in proving all of these charges before reluctant federal courts, there is ample evidence from other sources of a constitutional crisis. The history of covert operations prior to the Iran-contra scandal includes attempts to assassinate foreign leaders, successful ousters of democratic governments, cooperation with mafia-type figures and efforts to deceive the U.S. people and Congress. In government hearings on the Iran-contra affair it became clear that Admiral Poindexter and Lt. Col. Oliver North, cited earlier, both intentionally deceived Congress while carrying out an illegal war against Nicaragua on behalf of the National Security Council and the President. Former General John Singlaub, a key fundraiser for the contras, indicated that funds could be raised for the "freedom fighters" through secret three-way arms deals. "The United

States ... has at its disposal a large and continuous supply of Soviet technology and weapons to channel to the Freedom Fighters worldwide," Singlaub told CIA Director Casey in a memo, "mandating neither the consent or [sic] awareness of the Department of State or Congress." Such illegal methods were justified by Singlaub because "with each passing year, Congress has become increasingly unpredictable and uncooperative regarding the President's desire to support the cause of the Freedom Fighters."[13]

The means that we utilize in pursuit of various ends are a spiritual window into our own souls. This is as true for nations as for individuals. When the United States terrorizes civilians in its war to inflict suffering on the Nicaraguan people it reveals a profound deficiency or sickness within the nation's character. When verbal commitments to democracy are made a mockery of by actual practices, democracy is undermined at home and abroad. National self-deceit is no less hazardous than cancer symptoms in a person who decides to ignore the troubling symptoms rather than to receive appropriate treatment.

We have been far more successful at deceiving ourselves than others. For example, the depth and cynical nature of the U.S. war against the poor has been effectively hidden from the U.S. people as a whole. Self-deception has been aided by consumer comforts, an imperial presidency, a co-optable Congress, and an accommodating mainline press. However, overall efforts to manage images to mask the reality of U.S. arrogance and power and U.S.-sponsored terrorism have generally failed.

Many U.S. citizens support low-intensity-conflict strategy through the complicity of their silence but remain skeptical of U.S. intentions and policies. The United States has alienated traditional allies. The image and standing of the United States throughout Latin America has perhaps never been lower. David Steel, the head of Britain's Liberal party, charged the Reagan administration with "encouraging cross-border terrorism in Central America." A delegation of Western European parliamentarians wrote to President Reagan warning that "it has become increasingly difficult for elected officials throughout Europe to defend the NATO [North Atlantic Treaty Organization] alliance because of U.S. policy in Central America. A policy which makes a mockery of Western values," the letter continues, "which brazenly violates international law, which tramples over the very principles of the NATO charter only weakens the whole alliance."[14]

If the means through which the United States carries out its foreign policy are windows through which we can better see ourselves, then one can better understand why D'Escoto expressed concern about our well-being, the viability of our democracy, and the likelihood of widespread repression against U.S. citizens. I remember being impressed by the atmosphere of forgiveness I encountered in Nicaragua when I began regular visits to that country in 1982. The Nicaraguan revolution that ousted a bloody U.S.-backed dictatorship in 1979 was one of the first revolutions in history that was not followed by a vengeful bloodbath. The new Nicaraguan government immediately abolished the death penalty. When I asked Nicaraguan religious and political leaders why, in Nicaragua, there had not been mass executions of former Somoza collaborators, they said that the "spiritual costs to the revolution" would have been too high. There was a clear recognition that the relationship between means and ends is not simply one of expediency; that relationship determines who we are and what we shall become.

DEMOCRACY AND THE U.S. PRESS

I am frequently asked questions about the role of the U.S. press in relation to the widespread indifference to or ignorance about the human costs of U.S. foreign policy. How do the mainline print, radio, and television media shape how we think about ourselves as a people and as a nation? Why and how does the mainline media contribute to a deeply internalized worldview of the United States as a benevolent superpower rather than as an exploitative empire? Why does the press consistently portray the United States as a bold fighter against international terrorism while ignoring U.S.-sponsored terrorism in Central America and elsewhere? Why isn't low-intensity conflict a familiar concept to U.S. citizens, who are supposed to participate in a meaningful way in shaping their democracy, including their nation's foreign policy? Why is the U.S. war against the poor so hidden from public consciousness?

A detailed critique of the mainline U.S. media is available elsewhere and is beyond the scope of this book.[15] However, I offer these observations about the mainline media, which plays such an important role in shaping our understanding of the world and the role of the United States within it. The media is a critical actor in the war of images that is so central to low-intensity conflict. It is also instrumental in determining the quality of our democracy.

"If we live in a country with a free press," I asked myself many times while living in Central America, "then why are we so ignorant?" This question arose out of many discrepancies that I experienced: between stated and actual U.S. policy goals, between rhetoric about "freedom fighters" and terrorism against civilians, between press coverage of Nicaragua versus that of El Salvador, between the relative openness of U.S. citizens whose views on Central America had been shaped by experience or by alternative media sources versus the rather closed and arrogant perspectives of people whose sources of information were primarily television news and mainline papers and magazines such as *Time* and *Newsweek*.

There are no easy explanations as to why relatively well-educated people, living in a country with a "free press," are basically ignorant of or misinformed about the consequences of U.S. foreign policy. The following observations are offered with the hope that they will stimulate widespread discussion of the role of the media in shaping and oftentimes distorting our worldview.

First, within the United States, people have the right and the freedom to explore and to express a variety of perspectives on political events. This freedom is important and it should not be taken for granted. The problem is that for a variety of reasons this freedom is not or cannot be exercised by many citizens. Poor people in the United States, for example, rarely if ever have the opportunity to travel to Central America or other third-world countries. It is not possible for them to take a first-hand look at U.S. policies or at liberation struggles that might help inspire their own movements for social change. Others have been psychologically wounded by years of degrading poverty, including the indignity of unemployment and welfare. The largest and fastest-growing group of poor in the United States is the group of the working poor. Millions of poor working-class people have little time or energy to think about politics, particularly about foreign policy issues. Their thoughts and actions are focused on survival.

The attitudes of economically better-off citizens are shaped by the dominant culture's emphasis on individualism and consumerism. Those who travel are likely to be tourists in Europe. If people travel to Mexico or other third-world countries, it will most likely be to take advantage of beautiful beaches and favorable exchange rates rather than to explore the causes of hunger and poverty.[16] The majority of people, rich or poor, who actually follow the news rely heavily on major television networks and local newspapers. This means that although people have the right to explore a variety of perspectives on political issues, and good alternative sources of information are available for those with the time, energy, and commitment to use them, practically speaking the vast majority of U.S. citizens are exposed to a very narrow range of ideas.

Second, the U.S. press isn't really free if, by free, is meant that it is independent and without bias. The United States has a mainline press that is dominated by and reflects the interests of big money. The capacity of poorly funded alternative information networks seriously to challenge the dominant myths that are the foundation of empire is very limited. The reality is that people or groups with money are the major media. The institutions that make up the mainline press are not only sympathetic to big business; they *are* big business. What is fit to print is often determined indirectly by corporate advertisers or directly through outright ownership or control. Sociologist Michael Parenti in his book *Inventing Reality: The Politics of the Mass Media* writes:

> To maintain the system that is so good to them, the rich and powerful devote much attention to persuasion and propaganda. Control over the communication field and the flow of mass information, helps secure the legitimacy of the owning class's politico-economic power. We don't have a free and independent press in the United States but one that

is tied by purchase and persuasion to wealthy elites and their government counterparts.[17]

According to Parenti:

Ten business and financial corporations control the three major television and radio networks (NBC, CBS, ABC), 34 subsidiary television
stations, 201 cable TV systems, 62 radio stations, 20 record companies,
59 magazines including *Time* and *Newsweek*, 58 newspapers including
the *New York Times*, the *Washington Post,* the *Wall Street Journal*, and
the *Los Angeles Times*, 41 book publishers, and various motion picture
companies like Columbia Pictures and Twentieth-Century Fox. Three
quarters of the major stockholders of ABC, CBS and NBC are banks
such as Chase Manhattan, Morgan Guarantee Trust, Citibank, and
Bank of America.[18]

It is clearly not in the interests of the groups that lie behind the mainline
media to challenge the myth of the benevolent superpower, daily to document U.S. attempts to manage terrorism in Central America, or to report
sympathetically on the struggle of third-world peoples for self-determination. These are subjects to be avoided or distorted.

Third, U.S. government officials have the capacity to flood the media
with distorted information that effectively sets the parameters for debate
of crucial issues. The State Department holds a daily press briefing. The
White House and the Pentagon each hold two. The State Department and
the Pentagon each issue more than 600 press releases a year, while the
White House issues between 15 and 20 each day. Press releases and briefings
are supplemented by interviews, background papers, leaks, and a variety of
staged events. Referring to the success of U.S. government efforts to bias
press coverage against Nicaragua, the organization Fairness & Accuracy in
Reporting (FAIR) states: "By sheer force of repetition, the administration
has driven home its anti-Sandinista propaganda themes in the media. No
matter how outrageous the allegation," FAIR continues, "few reporters
bothered to include a simple disclaimer: 'The charge could not be independently verified.' "[19]

The media under the guise of "objective reporting" often serves as a
mouthpiece for U.S. government propaganda. The degree to which the press
accepts the parameters established by government officials can be illustrated
by press coverage of the Arias Peace Accords. The Arias plan required
each of the Central American countries to carry out simultaneously certain
reforms, including arranging cease fires with armed opposition groups, dialogue with internal opposition forces, preventing armed groups such as the
contras from operating from the territory of any Central American country,
press liberalization, and several other provisions. U.S. media coverage of
the Arias Peace Plan focused little or no attention on the compliance of

U.S.-backed governments often at war against their own people but did flood the U.S. people with information consistent with the administration's agenda.

Writer Alexander Cockburn did a search of available *New York Times* files over the five-and-one-half month period immediately following the signing of the peace accord. Although each country in Central America was required to comply with various provisions of the accord, Cockburn found "about 100 stories on Nicaragua's compliance with the accords; half a dozen on El Salvador's, two on Honduras' and none on Guatemala's."[20]Setting the parameters of the debate is a powerful way to influence and restrict discussion of critical issues. Once parameters have been narrowly set, the credibility of those who offer fundamental criticisms is in doubt. In general, it is acceptable to criticize a specific policy or to call attention to various problems as long as you do not violate the terms of the debate by focusing on causes or by challenging systems. Brazilian Archbishop Dom Helder Camara once said that when he gave food to the poor they called him a saint, but when he asked why people were poor they called him a communist.

The reluctance to overstep acceptable boundaries helps to explain why Democrats in the U.S. Congress or journalists who disagreed with U.S. support for the contras rarely if ever spoke about positive aspects of the Nicaraguan revolution or about Nicaragua's right to self-determination. The terms of the debate were clear: Nicaragua was "evil" and the United States had to take appropriate steps. Differences arose over what constituted appropriate steps.

Government- and press-determined boundaries have made the U.S. two-party system both dull and narrow in scope. U.S. voters must choose between a much more limited range of views and policy options compared to those offered by political parties in other Western democracies or in "totalitarian" Nicaragua for that matter. In Nicaragua seven political parties participated in the 1984 elections, including several to the left and to the right of the Sandinista party. U.S. government leaders and an "objective" press described the Sandinistas in Nicaragua as "communist," "Marxist," "Marxist/Leninist," "totalitarian," "Cuban-backed," or "Soviet-backed" so often that few U.S. citizens knew that Sweden was giving more aid to Nicaragua per capita than to any other country or that while Nicaragua does have both a Communist party and a Marxist-Leninist party these two parties together received less than 3 percent of the vote and are distinct from and hostile to the Sandinista party.

The U.S. political process is still deeply scarred from the purges and paranoia of the McCarthy period. The acceptance of boundaries that limit debate has become a form of self-censorship that distorts the information flow that is necessary for a well-informed citizenry, on which authentic democracy depends. Therefore, for political leaders and the mainstream press, capitalism is sacred and not to be criticized, socialism always fails, U.S. interventions in the third world are either justifiable or are "mistakes" that are well intentioned and exceptional, and abuses of power such as those of Watergate or the Iran-contra scandal are problems of individuals and not systems. The list could go on and on.

When someone like Raymond Bonner reports honestly about U.S.-sponsored terror in El Salvador for a major newspaper like the *New York Times*, he gets transferred to the financial pages. This has a chilling effect on other journalists who consciously or unconsciously learn that it is acceptable to criticize this or that policy but it is never acceptable to challenge the system that gives rise to that policy. *When it comes to evaluating systems, the only acceptable political stance for owners or journalists within the mainline press is a politics of assurance.* For example, in the Introduction to the Tower Commission Report [the Tower Commission was appointed by President Reagan to investigate the Iran-contra scandal], the chief Washington correspondent for the *New York Times*, R. W. Apple, Jr., describes the Iran-contra affair as "a pair of grievous missteps" which were not as serious as Watergate. "This is not a portrait of venality. It is a portrait of ineptitude verging on incompetence," Apple writes. "It is a portrait not of inadequate institutions but of stumbling, shortsighted stewardship of the national trust at a moment of crisis."[21]

The political landscape is also surrounded by ideological fences that confine debate within acceptable boundaries. With the possible exception of the challenging role played by Jesse Jackson in the Democratic primaries, Republicans and Democrats rarely pose radical challenges to deeply ingrained myths. Not surprisingly, Jackson was feared by the power brokers of his own party, who were hopeful he could bring new voters to the Democratic party but terrified that he might actually win the nomination for or the actual presidency. Michael Dukakis was so concerned about fitting within the ideological mainstream that he chose Lloyd Bentsen as his running mate even though they disagreed on nearly every major policy issue. The successful Republican campaign of red-baiting Dukakis as a "liberal" illustrates that the range of acceptable thought is extremely narrow. Political economist John Kenneth Galbraith notes how political conservatism benefits from

> the deep desire of politicians, Democrats in particular, for respectability—their need to show that they are individuals of sound confidence-inspiring judgment. And what is the test of respectability? It is, broadly, whether speech and action are consistent with the comfort and well-being of people of property and position. A radical is anyone who causes discomfort or otherwise offends such interests. Thus, in our politics, we test even liberals by their conservatism.[22]

Fourth, a fundamental bias against the poor tends to distort rather than illuminate reality in coverage in the mainline media. Powerful groups influence the media and they tend to see the rich and powerful as the newsmakers. Poor people rarely make the news other than as an occasional "human interest story" or as part of a series on "welfare cheats." One in five U.S. children are now born into poverty and the infant-mortality rate in parts of Detroit is higher than in Honduras, but the structural causes of poverty go unreported and remain invisible.

The White House has constant access to the media to issue diatribes against the Nicaraguan revolution. However, few stories are written from the perspective of poor Nicaraguan campesinos who received land in Nicaragua's agrarian reform, learned to read in the literacy crusade, and, as a consequence of the revolution, now send their children to local schools and health clinics. As United States low-intensity-conflict strategy succeeds in making life miserable for all Nicaraguans the press can be expected to report on economic hardship as evidence of the failure of the revolution without describing such hardship as the intent and result of United States policy. If Nicaragua's economic and social reforms are discussed in the U.S. press it is likely to be from the perspective of U.S. government officials or Nicaragua's business elites who speak English and are eager to talk to the press about "totalitarian" Nicaragua.

Finally, our relative ignorance about low-intensity conflict and the U. S. war against the poor has to do with sophisticated efforts to manage the news. We would be naive to think that our nation's capacity to distort and manage the news overseas would not be used at home. Bishop Pedro Casaldáliga in a poem about one of the international outlets for U. S. propaganda, the voice of America, writes:

> People should realize
> that this is the Voice of those who have a voice
> because they have their dollars
> and they have the power to kill, with a button,
> the whole human race
> and under their own roof the power
> to kill, day by day, with counterinformation
> their own sickly conscience.[23]

The United States, which extols the virtues of freedom of the press, regularly places foreign journalists — and, according to former CIA agent John Stockwell, has "many" U.S. journalists — on the CIA's payroll. The CIA funds books to influence U.S. public opinion without acknowledging CIA involvement. It also regularly plants false stories with overseas papers or wire services that often are later quoted in the U.S. media, without of course citing the CIA as the source of the information. The agency also fabricates events to justify U.S. interventionism. According to Ralph McGhee, who worked with the agency for more than twenty-five years: "where the necessary circumstances or proofs are lacking to support U.S.

intervention; the CIA creates the appropriate situations, or else invents them."[24]

In chapter 3, I indicated how disinformation is central to the low-intensity-conflict strategy of controlling the hearts and minds of the U.S. people. U.S. citizens are considered strategic targets in a war of images. The Reagan administration in 1984, consistent with this view, upgraded and renamed the State Department Office of Public Liaison (now called the Office of Public Diplomacy) to carry out "perception management operations."[25] According to documents released by the Iran-contra investigating committee, National Security Council members Oliver North and Walter Raymond directed efforts by the State Department's Office of Public Diplomacy to orchestrate negative news coverage of Nicaragua. The documents reveal how the National Security Agency leaked intelligence information, directed covert operations within Nicaragua to influence U.S. public opinion, and developed other elaborate programs for the diplomacy office to help the Reagan administration persuade Congress to renew contra aid. "If you look at it as a whole," a senior U.S. official, quoted in the *Miami Herald,* said, "the Office of Public Diplomacy was carrying out a huge psychological operation of the kind the military conducts to influence a population in denied or enemy territory."[26]

The National Security Council did not limit its disinformation efforts to the Office of Public Diplomacy. It also contracted with Robert Owen's public relations firm, I.D.E.A. Inc. Owen was a courier who shuttled back and forth between Washington and Central America with messages and money on behalf of the contras. He once said that giving aid to the contras was like "pouring money down a sinkhole." However, his agency accepted $50,000 earmarked by Congress for humanitarian assistance to the contras. I.D.E.A. Inc. carried out public relations campaigns on behalf of the contras, worked to set up a private citizen-operated contra support group, and helped to divert attention from the illegal CIA support for the contras.[27]

Robert Owen and the National Security Council were selling a positive image of the contras to the U.S. public even as they offered more-honest assessments among themselves. Owen in a memo to B.G., the initials of Oliver North's code name "Blood and Guts," said of the contra leadership: "Unfortunately, they are not first rate people: in fact they are liars and greed and power motivated. They are not the people to rebuild a new Nicaragua." In the same memo he indicated: "This war has become a business to many of them; there is still a belief the marines are going to have to invade so let's get set so we will automatically be the ones put into power."

The United States government has not formally censored the U.S. press except in times of formally declared war. This has led people to the faulty conclusion that the press in the United States is "free" and that the people of the United States therefore are a well-informed and objective people who can trust the words, intentions, and actions of elected and corporate officials. Michael Parenti describes how this view may be dangerous to our own freedoms:

> The structures of control within the U.S. media are different from the institutionalized formal censorship we might expect of a government-controlled press; they are less visible and more subtle, not monolithic yet hierarchical, transmitted to the many by those who work for the few, essentially undemocratic and narrow in perspective, tied to the rich and powerful but not totally immune to the pressures of an agitated public, propagandistic yet sometimes providing hard information that is intentionally or unintentionally revealing. . . .
>
> That we *think* the American press is a free and independent institution may only be a measure of our successful habituation to a subtler, more familiar form of suppression. The worst forms of tyranny — or certainly the most successful ones — are not those we rail against but those that so insinuate themselves into the imagery of our consciousness and the fabric of our lives as not to be perceived as tyranny.[28]

DEMOCRACY IN CRISIS

The U.S. war against the poor is a costly war. Its victims include people in far-off places who are distant enough from our lives so as to not trouble our consciences or challenge our basic worldview. U.S. citizens do not see the blood of Herbert Anaya or Nicaraguan land-reform workers on their hands. Most people who live relatively affluent lives remain politically on the sidelines while trusting in the essential viability and goodness of the U.S. democratic system.

Indifference and ignorance can be both comforting and dangerous. I believe that our democracy is in *serious crisis. We may be entering, or may in fact already have entered, a period in which democracy in the United States is more illusionary than real.* By pointing to present danger signs and speculating about the future of U.S. democracy I hope to shatter the complacency that binds many of us. I would rather risk being called an alarmist than deal with the consequences of being timid, just as I would rather alert my neighbors to the possibility of a fire based on seeing smoke than remain silent until flames engulf their entire house. Time will tell whether such fears about U.S. democracy are fully justified.

Low-intensity conflict is a totalitarianlike strategy that is incompatible with authentic democracy. Information, which is central to responsible citizenship, is distorted for political purposes both within exploited third-world countries and within the United States. If the United States is capable of using elections in El Salvador as part of a conscious strategy to undermine democracy, then it seems likely that something similar may be happening at home. Is there not a direct relationship between elections that mask the sources of real power in El Salvador and the existence of a "secret team" in the United States? Senator Daniel Inouye at the Iran-contra hearings described the network that had subverted the U.S. Constitution and carried out illegal foreign policy as "a shadowy government with its own air force, its own navy, its own fundraising mechanism and the ability to pursue its own ideas of the national interest, free from all checks and balances, and free from the law itself."[29]

During the Iran-contra hearings Oliver North had the following exchange with Senate Chief Counsel Arthur Liman:

COL. NORTH: The director [CIA Director William Casey] was interested in the ability to go to an existing, as he put it, off-the-shelf, self-sustaining, stand-alone entity, that could perform certain activities on behalf of the United States.
MR. LIMAN: Are you not shocked that the director of Central Intelligence is proposing to you the creation of an organization to do these kinds of things, outside of his own organization?
COL. NORTH: Counsel, I can tell you I'm not shocked.

Mr. Liman phrased his question in terms of a future possibility, but the "stand-alone entity" may already exist and may already have been operating for more than twenty-five years. It does not bode well for United States democracy that despite the Iran-contra hearings not one meaningful step has been taken to dismantle the shadow government.

There is also an important connection between reconsidering "long-standing American concepts of fair play," in pursuit of foreign enemies, as was recommended by the Hoover Report, and domestic spying and repression. Bill Moyers, in his report on *The Secret Government: The Constitution in Crisis*, says:

But the secret government had also waged war on the American people. The [Church] hearings examined a long train of covert actions at home, from the bugging of Martin Luther King by the FBI under Kennedy and Johnson, to gross violations of the law and of civil liberties in the 1970s. They went under code names such as Chaos, Cable Splicer, Garden Plot, and Leprechaun. According to the hearings, the secret government had been given a license to reach all the way to every mailbox, every college campus, every telephone and every home.[30]

Revelations of U.S. government infiltration of the Sanctuary movement and Federal Bureau of Investigation (FBI) harassment of organizations opposed to U.S. policy in Central America, such as CISPES (Committee in Solidarity with the People of El Salvador), are indications that the "license" has not yet expired. "It is imperative at this time," a statement from the FBI's file on CISPES says, "to formulate some plan of attack against

CISPES and specifically against individuals . . . who defiantly display their contempt for the U.S. government."

The U.S. government has the capacity to target the people of the United States with the sophisticated spy technology used against foreign enemies. The Iran-contra affair reveals that there are people in and outside of that government with the will to do so. After studying U.S. spy technology and documenting abuses by the CIA and the FBI up to the mid-1970s, Senator Frank Church concluded:

> At the same time, that capability at any time could be turned around on the American people and no American would have any privacy left, such [is] the capability to monitor everything: telephone conversations, telegrams, it doesn't matter. There would be no place to hide. If this government ever became a tyranny, if a dictator ever took charge in this country, the technological capacity that the intelligence community has given the government could enable it to impose total tyranny, and there would be no way to fight back, because the most careful effort to combine together in resistance to the government, no matter how privately it was done, is within the reach of the government to know. Such is the capability of this technology . . . . I don't want to see this country ever go across the bridge. I know the capacity that is there to make tyranny total in America, and we must see to it that this agency and all agencies that possess this technology operate within the law and under proper supervision, so that we never cross over that abyss. That is the abyss from which there is no return.[31]

Are we still on the bridge leading to the abyss or have we reached the other side? A people that allows its president to declare a national emergency within the United States in order to justify an economic embargo against the impoverished country of Nicaragua could easily lose its freedom. In April 1986, according to the Christic Institute lawsuit, President Reagan issued a top-secret National Security Decision Directive, which authorized the creation of ten military detention centers within the United States capable of housing 400,000 political prisoners. These detention centers were to be used "in the event that President Reagan chose to declare a 'State of Domestic National Emergency' concurrent with the launching of a direct United States military operation into Central America."[32] This was only one of at least 280 secret National Security Decision Directives issued by President Reagan.[33]

People who express unquestioning confidence in the U.S. democratic system place great faith in the U.S. electoral process and the "free press." Elections and lack of government censorship are cited as proof of the effectiveness of our democratic system. It seems important to remember, however, that low-intensity conflict is a war of images designed to obscure reality. In El Salvador the goal was to maintain control through more subtle forms of tyranny. Selective repression was preferred over generalized repression. Elections that served as a cover for real power were better than blatant dictatorship. Repression and tyranny were managed according to how much violence and intimidation were necessary to maintain control.

If images can obscure reality in El Salvador then they may also do so in the United States. The boundaries of our freedom have not been tested. An uninformed and largely passive populace has made overt repression less necessary in the United States. Journalists and politicians who consciously or unconsciously are skilled in the art of self-censorship have made harsher government measures to curb meaningful debate unnecessary.

If we wake from our slumber and build a movement capable of challenging the U.S. war against the poor, or if our historical situation changes significantly, then we will see if our democracy is in fact deeply rooted. Shadow governments subverting the U.S. Constitution, Salvadoran death squads operating in the United States, and presidential directives authorizing detention centers are indications that hard times may be on the horizon.[34]

The world that U.S. leaders will confront in the coming decades will likely be more unstable at home and abroad. The alternative to greater global justice is a "fortress America." Low-intensity-conflict strategy fails to address any of the real causes of social turmoil throughout the third world. Social tensions will continue to build and explode as economic injustice gives rise to movements for social change. The U.S. war against the poor will be an increasingly frustrating and costly proposition.

If there is a shift in the United States toward more overt forms of tyranny, it will likely be a response to a serious economic crisis. One ironic result of the U.S. war against the poor could be the collapse of the international economy. The inability of third-world countries either to pay their debts or to provide sufficient markets for goods produced in the United States or other industrial countries could contribute to a major worldwide depression.

The United States over the next several decades will face serious economic difficulties and an erosion of living standards even without an all-out collapse of the world economy. The Reagan presidency marked a turning point in recent U.S. history in which the United States shifted from being the world's largest creditor country to being the world's most indebted country. At the same time, record government deficits raised the national debt from about $900 billion in 1980 to more than $2 trillion in 1988. The people of the United States, guided by shortsighted leaders, have mortgaged the futures of many generations to come.

The political significance of a major economic crisis or significant economic decline is hard to predict with certainty. The relative affluence of many U.S. citizens has tended to cover up or mask serious problems of racism and antagonism between social classes. Already during the Reagan presidency decisions were made about how to divide up limited resources. Not surprisingly, the poor were big losers as savings from cuts in social programs were used to feed an unprecedented military buildup and offset tax breaks for the rich. Increased military spending contributed to the deficit, and its emphasis on nonproductive growth was a major factor in the declining competitive position of the United States in world trade.

Austerity programs similar to those imposed on third-world countries by the International Monetary Fund may soon be required of the United States. When this happens the poor will be further victimized and U.S. economic elites can be expected to use racism and ideological campaigns blaming the victim to take attention away from their own role in managing a crisis in defense of their own interests. The political climate could turn nasty as the United States intervenes throughout the third world in order to block meaningful reforms while at the same time it confronts growing social turmoil at home.

The U.S. war against the poor may one day come home with a vengeance. The result could be a more visible tyranny including dictatorship, even fascism. The June 1988 issue of *Success* magazine described the drastic measures that were necessary to rescue floundering companies. An article entitled "Ruthless Leaders" was about "The Brutal Men Who Slash Divisions, Fire Employees, and Save Companies." There may be frightening parallels between the article's justification of tyranny to save a failing company and a broader corporate response to a major national economic crisis:

> A company is staggering toward death. Management has taken some steps to stave off decline. . . .Can this company be saved from bankruptcy and oblivion?
>
> The board calls for help, and brings in a turnaround artist. He's a corporate drill sergeant: plain spoken and unafraid — a specialist in kicking a flabby company into a shape that will make money.
>
> The turnaround artist is a . . . fiery, flamboyant loner who isn't afraid to make sweeping changes and brutal decisions. He is the unwelcome interloper who fires executives, lays off workers, and sells or closes divisions — regardless of the personal grief that results, the careers that are ruined, the reputations that are swept away.
>
> Like a ship's captain, the leader must be ruthless, even dictatorial. In the first months of the crisis, he orders more and more baggage overboard, allowing no questions, no hesitation . . . . [As one turnaround artist] put it when he first came aboard, "Until we turn profitable, something akin to martial law will be in effect."
>
> "I bust asses," one said to me. "I make the men sweat blood," said another. Most admit they use fear to motivate managers and workers to exceed past performances.[35]

The religious right can be expected to provide a theological justification for a tyrannical response to political or economic crises. The sons and daughters of the empire will once again rally around the flag, turn the cross on its side, and use it as a sword in an ongoing war against the poor. Television evangelist James Robison believes God will one day lift up a tyrannical leader in order to protect the American way of life. God will send a tyrant in order to confront the "communist propaganda and infiltration" that are linked to "satanic forces," which are attacking the United States. "Let me tell you something about the character of God," Robison told a group of pastors at a training session on how to mobilize congregations for conservative political causes. "If necessary, God would raise up a tyrant, a man who might not have the best ethics, to protect the freedom interests of the ethical and the godly."[36]

Religious support for tyranny seriously distorts Christian faith. It demonstrates how Christians living in an empire can be easily co-opted and how the gospel's liberating message can be perverted and placed at the service of the empire.

5

Faith and Empire

Empires no longer suit the race of human beings. . . . You may think you're the owners, you may have everything, even god, your god — the bloodstained idol of your dollars . . . but you don't have the God of Jesus Christ, the Humanity of God!

I swear by the blood of His Son, killed by another empire, and I swear by the blood of Latin America — now ready to give birth to new tomorrows — that you will be the last . . . emperor!

"Ode to Reagan," Bishop Pedro Casaldáliga

This is the mission entrusted to the church, a hard mission: to uproot sins from history, to uproot sins from the political order, to uproot sins from the economy, to uproot sins wherever they are. What a hard task! It has to meet conflicts amid so much selfishness, so much pride, so much vanity, so many who have enthroned the reign of sin among us.

Archbishop Oscar Romero

INTRODUCTION

Christians living in the United States are children of an empire. This is not our calling but it is the starting point for our journey in faith. We have deeply internalized the values of empire. Our acceptance of the culture's definition of freedom as the right of the powerful to invest and the right of the affluent to make consumer choices has preempted our freedom in Jesus Christ to be living signs of God's kingdom. We know little about low-intensity conflict, our country's global war against the poor, or the precarious position of our own democracy. We therefore lack a sense of the historical rootedness that is essential for a dynamic, living faith.

The U.S. empire is held together by deeply ingrained myths that serve as a buffer between the conscience of our people and the oppression of the poor. "Real criticism begins in the capacity to grieve because that is the most visceral announcement that things are not right," theologian Walter Brueggemann writes. "Only in the empire are we pressed and urged and invited to pretend that things are all right . . . . And as long as the empire can keep the pretense alive that things are all right, there will be no real grieving and no serious criticism."[1]

The U.S. empire engages in comforting doublespeak in order to discourage us from grieving, envisioning alternative futures, or offering meaningful criticisms. The empire talks about peace in order to cover its bloody tracks of war and war preparation; it espouses democracy but holds elections for undemocratic purposes, shields shadow governments from public scrutiny and destabilizes democracies that represent the interests of the poor; it "defends" human rights while funding and managing terrorism; it uses the existence of a "free press" as a yardstick to measure authentic democracies while engaging in disinformation campaigns and paying foreign and domestic journalists to be messengers of propaganda; and it condemns totalitarianism while secretly authorizing construction of detention centers and engaging in low-intensity conflict, a totalitarianlike strategy designed to control the hearts, minds, political choices, and economic destinies of people.

It isn't surprising that empires are capable of oppression, violence, and deceit. Empires, after all, are empires whether or not they use the adjective "evil" to describe their adversaries and "benevolent" to describe themselves. What is surprising and most disturbing is that Christians living in the United States have so thoroughly embraced imperial myths. We have accepted almost without question that capitalism is good, socialism is evil, flags belong in churches, the U.S. press is free and objective, widespread discrepancies between rich and poor are inevitable and somehow compatible with Christian faith, our nation's foreign policy is well intentioned, the underdevelopment of third-world peoples is unrelated to our own development, and democracy in the United States is exemplary, safe, and secure.

Our acceptance of and assimilation into empire has distorted our basic worldview and actions. It has co-opted our faith, sapped us of moral integrity, and left us subservient to a dominant ideology and culture. "The contemporary American church," Brueggemann notes, "is so largely enculturated to the American ethos of consumerism that it has little power to believe or to act."[2] As a measure of how distorted faith can become in the midst of empire, one need only recall James Robison's assertion that God will bless the United States with a tyrant.

The historical context of the United States is that of empire, but our calling as people of faith is to become the sons and daughters of God. To be faithful to our calling inevitably leads to a confrontation with the empire and the gods it calls on for legitimacy.

READING SCRIPTURE AS A CALL TO CONVERSION

By accident of birth or as part of God's plan, we are living in an empire in crisis. In order to find clues for our faith journey, Christians must pay particular attention to biblical stories that confront, threaten, or challenge people of power, people for whom God's word is first a word of judgment and perhaps later one of possibility.

Our fundamental error as Christians is that we allow the biblical word to conform to the dominant culture and thereby rob it of its capacity for liberation. This helps explain why most Christians and churches in the United States are indifferent to or ignorant of the U.S. war against the poor. The empire and its gods are fearful of honest words that condemn the structures of oppression or hopeful words that promise liberation.

The gospel is distorted within the empire because the "good news" is full of pain and promise. For the rich and powerful the good news is almost always a call to conversion. By removing the pain and promise from Scripture, we restrict our capacity to grieve, deny the need for repentance, and undermine the possibility of conversion. Faith is reduced to an afterlife insurance policy, paid in full through the blood of our resurrected Lord, and guaranteed by grace. Repentance, conversion, and salvation become words without historical significance.

Poor people engaged in liberation struggles find hope, strength, and courage in biblical texts and stories in which God expresses solidarity with their struggle. God's commitment to justice and to overcoming the structures of sin are expressed in texts such as the following:

Then the Lord said, "I have seen the affliction of my people who are in Egypt, and have heard their cry because of their taskmasters; I know their sufferings, and I have come down to deliver them out of the hand of the Egyptians, and to bring them up out of that land to a good and broad land, a land flowing with milk and honey . . ." [Exodus 3:7–8].

The Spirit of the Lord is upon me, because he has anointed me to preach good news to the poor. He has sent me to proclaim release to the captives and recovering of sight to the blind, to set at liberty those who are oppressed, to proclaim the acceptable year of the Lord [Luke 4:18–19].

For consider your call, [brothers and sisters]; not many of you were wise according to worldly standards, not many were powerful, not many were of noble birth; but God chose what is foolish in the world to shame the wise, God chose what is weak in the world to shame the strong, God chose what is low and despised in the world, even things that are not, to bring to nothing things that are, so that no human being might boast in the presence of God [1 Corinthians 1:26–29].

These texts reveal that compassion, justice, and concern for the well-being of the poor are central aspects of the character of God. In the exodus event God enters into history in a new and decisive way. The old social order and its gods lose their legitimacy. Jesus underscores God's commitment to overcoming the structures of sin by announcing his ministry as good news to the poor and by proclaiming the "acceptable year of the Lord," a likely reference to land reform within the context of the jubilee year. The passage from Corinthians reveals how God's priorities are dramatically different than those of empire. It is the poor and the weak who are special instruments of the kingdom.

These texts, obviously good news to the poor, also speak to us as children of empire. However, for these passages to engage us fully we must look at them through the eyes of those who would have been our contemporaries: the Pharaoh and his taskmasters, those responsible for the oppression that Jesus sets out to overcome, and the "wise and powerful ones" who look down upon the poor.

Like Pharaoh's subjects, we today are lined up and armed with ideological and military weapons to prevent others from passing through the wilderness toward freedom. Like servants and soldiers of a modern-day Caesar, we witness and knowingly or unknowingly participate in the crucifixion of millions of poor people throughout the third world. Hunger, poverty, and repression are the crosses they bear. All-knowing and profoundly arrogant, we look at the poor in Central America as "enemies" who live in "our backyard."

Christian acceptance of structural injustice and indifference to the human costs of low-intensity conflict are signs that the empire has co-opted our faith and is using religion to serve imperial goals. The empire's view of the poor clashes sharply with the God of the exodus and Jesus' portrayal of the kingdom. The poor who look to Scripture and claim God as their advocate are victimized by a war in defense of the U.S. empire. Once defined as enemies, the poor become troublesome waste products within an unjust global economy that extracts wealth from God's creation for the benefit of the few. From the perspective of faith the death of the poor through hunger and malnutrition represents the ongoing crucifixion of Jesus. According to the great judgment story in Matthew 25 when we feed the hungry we feed Jesus, when we clothe the naked we clothe Jesus, and it would be fair to say, when we wage war against the poor through low-intensity conflict we are at war against Jesus.

The passages above and the biblical message in general are good news to us only if we decide that following a liberating God is worth abandoning the unjust privileges that the empire delivers or promises to deliver. God's liberating, hope-filled message to the poor calls the rich and powerful to conversion.

ULTIMATE ALLEGIANCES

The central religious problem throughout the Bible is idolatry, not atheism. The biblical writers understand that all people have gods that demand ultimate allegiances. "For all the peoples walk each in the name of its god," Micah 4:5 says, "but we will walk in the name of the Lord our God for ever and ever." It is not accidental that when the prophets speak against social injustice they condemn the religious leaders, systems, and ceremonies that serve the unjust order:

> For from the least to the greatest of them, every one is greedy for unjust gain; and from prophet to priest, every one deals falsely. They have healed the wound of my people lightly saying, "Peace, peace," when there is no peace [Jeremiah 6:13–14].

> I hate, I despise your feasts, and I take no delight in your solemn assemblies. Even though you offer me your burnt offerings and cereal offerings, I will not accept them, and the peace offerings of your fatted beasts I will not look upon. Take away from me the noise of your songs: to the melody of your harps I will not listen. But let justice roll down like waters and righteousness like an ever-flowing stream [Amos 5:21–24].

There is an inevitable clash between a liberating God and empire. The first commandment, "You shall have no other gods before me," is prefaced with a reminder that the God who is to be worshiped and followed is the liberating God who broke with the religious and social order of empire: "I am the Lord your God, who brought you out of the land of Egypt, out of the house of bondage" (Deuteronomy 5:6). In Luke 4, as I mentioned earlier, Jesus' ministry and proclamation of the kingdom is consistent with the liberating God of the exodus. Jesus declares his ministry, which ultimately led the empire to crucify him, as "good news to the poor," "release to the captives," and liberty to the "oppressed" after he resisted temptations of national fame, wealth, and power (Luke 4:1–13). The early Christians facing both religious and political persecution summarized their resistance to idolatry by asserting that "Christ is Lord."

The freedom of God is a challenge to empires who use political power to oppress others. God's freedom to act on behalf of the oppressed challenges the well-ordered societies of Pharaohs and kings where the rich and the poor and comforting gods all know their places. Whether it be Moses confronting Egypt's Pharaoh, Jesus challenging Caesar's Rome, or the people of Nicaragua and El Salvador—inspired by a liberating theology—defying Washington, D.C., empires always resist alternative religious and political models that challenge their authority and privileges.

Walter Brueggemann notes that "the ministry of Moses" represents "a radical break with the social reality of Pharaoh's Egypt." In this radical break from "imperial reality," Moses "dismantles the politics of oppression and exploitation by countering it with a *politics of justice and compassion*" and he dismantles the empire's static religion "by exposing the gods and showing that in fact they had no power and were not gods." According to Brueggemann, the "mythic claims of the empire are ended by the disclosure of *the alternative religion of the freedom of God*."[3]

The good news from the exodus to the Jesus story to present-day El Salvador and Nicaragua is that God enters history and invalidates both empire and the religious idolatry that makes it possible. As followers of this liberating, myth-shattering, justice-oriented God, our task is to be living examples of meaningful alternatives. "The participants in the Exodus found themselves," Brueggemann writes, "undoubtedly surprisingly to them, involved in the intentional formation of a *new social community* to match the vision of God's freedom."[4]

Paul Hanson, in his book *The People Called: The Growth of Community in the Bible*, finds the search for authentic community to be the heart of the biblical narrative. The Bible in all its diversity describes the interaction between a liberating God and people of faith who seek to order their life in a manner consistent with God's compassion and freedom:

> The first event recorded in the Bible that can be called "historical" — the exodus — presents a mixed company . . . of people challenging the . . . orthodoxy of their time. They did so on the basis of real experiences that broke the credibility of the official religion of special privilege and that initiated a search for a radically different grounding for life. The resulting movement from hopeless slave bondage into freedom gave birth to a notion of community dedicated to the ordering of *all* life, for the good of *all* life, under the guidance and empowerment of a righteous, compassionate God.
>
> This notion, unlike the one it challenged, did not offer a finished program; it inaugurated a process. It did not commend to its members static answers; it offered the perspective of those who had experienced deliverance to others who suffered under various kinds of oppression . . . . Taken as a whole, it manifested a purpose dedicated to the redemption and restoration of the entire created order.[5]

Idolatry is the inevitable consequence of Christians' tolerating or conforming to the values, myths, and rewards of empire. Empires demand ultimate allegiances. By allowing ourselves to be subservient to the U.S. empire, our lifestyles and political priorities are indistinguishable from other citizens. Assimilation into the dominant culture makes it impossible for us to help construct an alternative social order more consistent with the compassion of God. Religion serves the empire rather than the God of liberation and justice. Our capacity to be a creative leaven within society is buried beneath an avalanche of rewards doled out by the empire, including comforting myths, nationalistic slogans, consumer goods, and power.

OUR CONFESSIONAL SITUATION

The community of faith must be clear about ultimate allegiances in all times and in all places. There is no possibility of authentic faith if we forget the first commandment or fail to assert in word and deed that "Christ is Lord." The biblical writers' perspective on the role and acceptability of government evolved over time. In general, the institution of government is seen as a gift from God. However, not all governments or actions of specific governments are to be obeyed. Governments are to be judged in light of a justice-seeking God, and national citizenship is for Christians always provisional.[6]

There are some situations, such as the persecution and death of Jews in Nazi Germany, which *require* Christians to resist government authorities. Neutrality in situations such as these is impossible. We are required to affirm publicly the Lordship of Christ, denounce injustice, confess our complicity with evil, acknowledge our need for forgiveness, and take costly action.

The U.S. war against the poor presents Christians in the United States with such a situation. The world economy is structured so that the poor experience hunger, poverty, and hopelessness while the rich enjoy luxuries and power. German theologian Ulrich Duchrow, in his book *Global Economy: A Confessional Issue for the Churches*, describes how injustice within the present world economy is as serious an affront to Christian faith as apartheid or the atrocities of the Third Reich:

> My question is whether apartheid is not just the tip of the iceberg. We inhabitants of industrialized nations, together with a few tiny elites in the countries of Asia, Africa and Latin America, are exploiting the majority of the world's population just as systematically as the white South Africans exploit the majority of the people in South Africa. The demon of profit for the few at the expense (i.e. the impoverishment) of the many has the whole world economic system firmly in its grip, with all the side-effects in the shape of discrimination and the suppression of human rights. The forty million or more deaths from starvation per year, the direct result of the workings of the present global economic system, require of us just as clear a confession of guilt as did the murder of the six million Jewish men, women and children in Nazi Germany and as does the deprivation of twenty million people in South Africa of their rights today.[7]

The injustice structured into the global economy would in itself justify Christians in the leading capitalist power to view the present situation as a confessional moment. It is long past time for Christians worldwide to denounce hunger as unacceptable to God and to the human family. Martin

Luther, in his commentary on the commandment "Thou shalt not kill," says that "all those who fail to offer counsel and aid to people in need, to those in physical danger even of death, God rightly calls 'murderers'.... You may not have actually committed all these crimes but you have for your part left your neighbor to pine and die in distress."[8]

Our confessional moment becomes more urgent by virtue of the fact that we are not only fully integrated into this global economy, we are also living in a nation that is fighting a sophisticated yet undeclared war against the poor. The United States seeks to defend its privileged position within the unjust world economy through low-intensity conflict. It uses deceit, terror, intimidation, and secrecy; defines suffering as victory; and punishes people and governments that are committed to redistributing power and resources to meet the needs of the poor.

Francis Boyle, professor of international law at the University of Illinois, accurately states our ethical dilemma:

> Forty years ago at Nuremberg, representatives of the United States government participated in the prosecution and punishment of Nazi government officials for committing some of the same types of international crimes that members of the Reagan administration today are inflicting upon the civilian population. The American people must reaffirm our commitment to the *Nuremberg Principles* by holding their government officials fully accountable under international and U.S.
>
> We must not permit any aspect of our foreign affairs and defense We must not permit any aspect of our foreign affairs and defense policies to be conducted by acknowledged "war criminals" according to the U.S. government's own official definition of that term. At the very minimum, the American people must insist upon the impeachment, dismissal or resignation of all Reagan administration officials responsible for complicity in the commission of international crimes in Nicaragua.

Reagan administration officials were not impeached for their crimes against the Nicaraguan people and their violation of the Nuremberg Principles. That does not lessen the severity of the crimes committed and it adds weight to our responsibility as Christians because of our complicity. Confession must begin with people of faith and with church institutions. We cannot rightfully expect or hope for national repentance or conversion without purging ourselves of the values, lifestyles—both as individual Christians and as churches—and expectations of empire. "Our major problem fifty years ago," writes Eberhard Bethge in the foreword to Duchrow's *Global Economy*, "was not so much the wickedness and godlessness of the Nazis. Our problem then was the fanatical or deceitful falsification and corruption of the substance of the Christian faith and the devastation this wrought on the life and witness of the people of God."

In *Saying Yes and Saying No* theologian Robert McAfee Brown writes that his "greatest fear" is that the United States might "slide down [the] slippery slope" to "fascism with a friendly face." "The greatest failure of the church" in Nazi Germany "was *to wait too long* before engaging in significant protest." The great challenge facing churches in the United States, according to Brown, "is to avoid that failure and to speak loudly and clearly at the first telltale signs of national idolatry, so that its development can be arrested before it is too late."[9]

My greatest fears are that Christians in the United States will continue to live out their faith as if 40 million people dying each year from hunger is normal, acceptable, or necessary, and that we shall fail to see a connection between our distorted faith and the ability of the nation's leaders to carry on a global war against the poor utilizing low-intensity conflict. These fears lead me to call on Christians and churches to denounce the evil and *to confess our complicity with sinful structures because the suffering outside our national borders is already sufficient to demand confession.* Also, a failure to confess our participation in social injustice, our subservience to the dominant culture, and our idolatry before the national gods of wealth and power will inevitably lead to internal repression, an erosion of democratic freedoms, or a "slippery slide" toward fascism, friendly or otherwise.

THE CONTENT OF CONFESSION

In the *Lutheran Book of Worship* there is a "brief order for confession and forgiveness," which includes the following words

> [PASTOR:] If we say we have no sin, we deceive ourselves, and the truth is not in us. But if we confess our sins, God who is faithful and just will forgive our sins and cleanse us from all unrighteousness. Most merciful God . . .
> [CONGREGATION:] . . . we confess that we are in bondage to sin and cannot free ourselves. We have sinned against you in thought, word, and deed, by what we have done and by what we have left undone. We have not loved you with our whole heart; we have not loved our neighbors as ourselves. For the sake of your Son, Jesus Christ, have mercy on us. Forgive us, renew us, and lead us, so that we may delight in your will and walk in your ways, to the glory of your holy name. Amen[10]

These words of confession are an important acknowledgment of our need for forgiveness. However, it is the task of us as individual Christians, and of our churches, to be more specific about the sins we commit or participate in through our action or inaction. By naming or confessing our sins more concretely we begin to lessen the power sin has to distort our lives. We open up the possibility of lived repentance, that is, a reordering of our values, priorities, and actions to be more consistent with our faith in a compassionate, justice-seeking God.

In this book I have argued that the U.S. war against the poor is so insidious, so much in conflict with authentic democracy and Christian faith that it requires Christians to take bold action. The U.S. war against the poor and its strategy of low-intensity conflict is so broad in scope, so cynical in outlook, so damaging in practice that it presents Christians and churches in the United States with a historical challenge similar to that faced by the Confessing churches in Nazi Germany. A confessional situation demands acknowledgment of our participation in sinful social structures, repentance, and creative action.

The content of our confession, in light of low-intensity conflict and the U.S. war against the poor, will need to include elements such as the following:

First, we need to confess that, despite verbal commitments to the contrary, our actions indicate a confusion over ultimate allegiances. Most Christians and churches in the United States are guilty of idolatry. Our ultimate commitment is no longer to the God of community, compassion, and justice. Wealth, power, nationalism, and not Jesus Christ, have become lords of our lives. There is no greater task lying before Christians and our churches than to reassert our freedom in Christ. This freedom, which is rooted in faith, could make it possible for us to overcome our subservience to the dominant culture and be a light and leaven to the United States and to the world.

In order to clarify our ultimate allegiance to Christ and to separate ourselves from the dominant culture, we must stop living as if these are normal times. Forty million people dying from hunger-related causes cannot be regarded as normal. A global economy that worships the idol of the "free market" and leaves the poor increasingly desperate is unacceptable. The use of terrorism by the United States in Central America, defining suffering as victory, using elections for undemocratic purposes, tolerating the death of the poor through international finance, concealing the existence of shadow governments, issuing presidential decrees to construct detention centers for political prisoners, and implementing the totalitarianlike strategy of low-intensity conflict call us to immediate and bold action.

One tactic we can use as we wrestle to free ourselves *from* the clutches of the dominant culture and *for* the gospel is noncooperation with evil. Tax resistance, refusal or withdrawal from military service or military or other socially unconscionable employment, distinctive lifestyles that withdraw from the neurosis of endless consumption and involve sharing and fulfillment of basic needs are possible steps leading to independence from national idols.

Second, we need to confess that our subservience to the idols of wealth and power, nationalism and capitalism has led us to ignore or to destroy the unity of the global body of Christ. Faith in a compassionate God that desires health and wholeness for the whole human family must necessarily transcend national boundaries. Ulrich Duchrow reflects upon the relationship between an unjust global economy and the universal body of Christ:

> ... participation in the body of Christ excludes systematic oppression and exploitation of certain groups of people within the church or in society generally.
>
> Some theologians ... are seeking in the light of the New Testament doctrine of the body of Christ to understand, analyze and influence the international economic processes and mechanisms which experience shows are already catastrophic in their effects and are becoming increasingly so with each passing day. ... The northern industrial countries ... are growing steadily richer at the expense of the majority of the people in the countries supplying the raw materials, who are becoming steadily poorer. ... Christians and churches in the "North" enjoy their growing (or at least protected) prosperity in part at least at the expense of the Christians and churches in the countries supplying the raw materials. In other words, *if we are in any real sense still the one universal body of Christ, this body of Christ is divided among active thieves, passive profiteers, and deprived victims* [italics added].[11]

Affirming the unity of the global body of Christ is an essential task that lies before us as individual Christians, as faith communities, and as churches. Groups like Witness for Peace, which have documented U.S.-sponsored terrorism and walked with the Nicaraguan people in their suffering, help show the way. So too do churches and church workers who challenge their nation's violation of domestic and international laws by offering sanctuary to refugees fleeing U.S.-sponsored terror in Central America. In El Salvador Christians from the United States have helped build international faith ties through material aid, spiritual support, and political solidarity. Christians and churches in the United States, in order to affirm our essential unity in the body of Christ, will need to become outspoken and active critics of the global economy, advocates of an alternative order including debt relief and fairer terms of trade, and determined resisters against low-intensity conflict.

Third, we need to confess that there is a relationship between our relative affluence and our willingness to accept imperial myths and to ignore or be indifferent to U.S. foreign and domestic policies that victimize the poor. The biblical writers frequently warn of the dangers of wealth and affluence. This is true both because wealth is often earned by exploiting the poor and because wealth tends to distort the worldview and faith perspective of those who are affluent. Jesus warns that it is impossible to serve both God and riches.

Our relative comfort helps explain our lack of interest in global problems. Indifference is the best friend of tyranny and injustice. *The desire not to know is as important as disinformation or a biased press in creating a broad climate of indifference and ignorance within U.S. churches and the society as a whole*. The lifestyles of most Christians and their churches fully reflect the goals and values of the dominant culture. Churches, pastors, and denominational executives are often locked into the prestige and indebtedness of comfortable salaries, large buildings, and hefty mortgages. They are often more concerned about how well the stock market is doing and in preserving the well-being of their pension and investment funds than they are about wars against the poor. Such preoccupations make following Jesus impossible.

The confessional situation confronts individual Christians, congregations, and denominational institutions with the need to overcome our addiction to power and privilege. Jesus, who embraced the alternative power of the cross, is calling us to take religious, political, and financial risks, and to seek alternative institutional forms. We cannot remain a church that is subservient to the powerful and be faithful to Jesus Christ. Our society and our brothers and sisters throughout the third world can no more tolerate the self-censorship of the churches than they can tolerate the self-censorship of the press. Both mainline churches and media sources have all too often internalized and projected a role as the guardians of empire through a politics of assurance. Pain and promise must be rediscovered in the Scriptures and echoed from the pulpits. Our complacency must be shattered, injustice denounced, and our call to conversion heard clearly, first in the churches and then within the society as a whole.

The lifestyles of individual Christians are also in need of transformation. Our addiction to the consumer society gives legitimacy to the unjust power and privilege of the dominant culture. John Francis Kavanaugh writes in his book *Following Christ in a Consumer Society*:

> Possessions which might otherwise serve as *expressions* of our humanity, and enhance us as persons, are transformed into ultimates. Our being is in having. Our happiness is said to be in possessing more. Our drive to consume, bolstered by an economics of infinite growth, becomes addictive; it moves from manipulated need, to the promise of joy in things, to broken promises and frustrated expectation, to guilt and greater need for buying. Property is no longer instrumental to our lives; it is the final judge of our merit. So vast in its pre-eminence, it is worth killing for.[12]

U.S. government and corporate leaders are willing to kill and to wage war against the poor in order to defend our "national valuables" from "have-not" peoples. Meanwhile, events such as the widespread drought during the summer of 1988 have renewed speculation that our mindless consumption may be causing irreversible damage to the environment. The consumer culture not only fosters indifference to the plight of the poor and our participation in their suffering; it also, in effect, is a war against future generations because it threatens to undermine the support base for all life.

Alternative lifestyles are essential for individual Christians and their churches. We must be living signs that wars against the poor are incompatible with Christian faith. Our voices will lack credibility and be without integrity unless we demonstrate our willingness to leave behind styles of living that are built on the blood and backs of the poor, and which are maintained at the expense of both present and future generations.

Alternative lifestyles need to be embraced for a variety of reasons: for the sake of personal and institutional credibility; as examples of how the "abundant life" is possible, perhaps only possible, when we are free from the illusionary pursuit of finding our meaning through having an endless consumption; as signs of joyful accommodation to a future in which the world's goods will be more evenly distributed to meet the basic needs of the whole human family; to share or give back resources that we have indirectly stolen through unjust economic structures; to offer resistance to sophisticated interventions on behalf of privilege through low-intensity conflict; to express solidarity with future generations and with the majority of the human family, which today has no choice about lifestyles; to increase our reliance on communities of people; and to break the endless cycle of consumption and indebtedness so that our time and our human talents can be devoted to building an alternative future more consistent with our faith in a compassionate, loving God.

Fourth, we confess that our subservience to the empire has eroded our capacity for hope, our ability to envision an alternative future, and our faith in the resurrection. I discussed earlier how the U.S. war against the poor is a war against hope: psychological warfare seeks to control people's hearts and minds; terrorism intimidates and destroys bodies and spirits; defining victory in terms of suffering leads to immoral and illegal actions to destroy the Nicaraguan revolution so that the poor in neighboring countries will understand the resolve of the empire and the consequences of seeking self-determination.

At the same time, as Walter Brueggemann stated earlier, the empire seeks to prevent us from grieving by offering us assurances that things are "O.K." We are told repeatedly by political and economic leaders and by the dominant culture that alternative futures are not necessary or possible. We are pacified through comforting ideologies and promises of fulfillment through consumption. Our failure to grieve atrophies our capacity for hope and healing just as terminal patients who deny their death never come to terms with the dying process.

There are alternatives to affluence at the expense of the poor, to fortress America, and to the drift away from democracy toward tyranny. The typical male paradigm for power is a situation in which there must be winners and losers. It is true that there is little chance of overcoming poverty without redistributing wealth and power. If poverty is caused by a lack of democracy, then more power for the poor will mean less power for those of us who are relatively rich. However, it may be that this redistribution of power is necessary for the well-being of the entire human family. In the Gospel of Mark, Jesus responds to a rich young man's question about eternal life by telling him to go and sell all he has and give it to the poor. Mark prefaces Jesus' troublesome directive with these words: "And Jesus looking upon him loved him, and said to him . . ." (Mark 10:21). Jesus' message to the young man was motivated by love. The rich man, unable to hear the good news in the message, walked away from Jesus' attempt to save him. The rich young man, like ourselves and our society, did not face a win/lose situation. However, he was unable to see that Jesus was interested in his well-being as much as the well-being of the poor.

The existence of wealth alongside massive hunger, poverty, and economic injustice is a sign of spiritual brokenness that desperately needs healing. Economic inequality and injustice demonstrate a lack of compassion and the need for transformation and healing of *both* the rich and the poor. Without transformation of the existing structures of violence and inequality, the male power paradigm of win or lose is ultimately a situation in which everyone loses. The shifting of power from the rich to the poor is necessary for the liberation of both rich and poor. It is ironic that the rich so consistently and ruthlessly seek to block the liberation of the poor on which their own redemption depends.

Our capacity to hope for and work for an alternative future must be rooted in faith and community. The dominant culture stresses individualism. People of faith must learn to find courage in community with others. Individuals will nearly always be overwhelmed by structural evil. The question "What can I do?" when asked alone is far more overwhelming than the question "What can we do?" asked in the context of a caring community of faith. Hope is rooted in honest assessments that enable both grieving and dreaming of new possibilities, in commitment and trust in others, in faith in God's faithfulness to us, in humor and urgency, in patience, endurance, and action.

The people of Central America teach us that a resurrection faith is possible only in community. Why are so few Christians and churches in the United States willing to take risks in order to denounce injustice and express solidarity in word and action with suffering people? One part of the answer to this question is the absence of community. People in Central America have a resurrection faith, that is, they refuse, as Jesus did, to let fear of death intimidate them into subservience to empire. They are part of communities of prayer, study, reflection, and action. They know that Jesus was crucified because he lived out his faith in a justice-loving God to its ultimate consequence, and they see suffering as a likely consequence of following Jesus' example. However, they have the capacity to take risks because their actions are rooted in community. If they should die or be persecuted or imprisoned as a consequence of living their faith, they know that the community of which they are a part will carry on their work and even be strengthened by the courage of their example. Because they are rooted in community, and many of us are not, they know that the risks they take will mean something, whereas we live with the gnawing fear that disrupting our lives may not be worth the trouble.

Finally, a word of personal confession. I do not know how to live in response to the confessional situation I have presented in this book. At times I feel overwhelmed by the evil of low-intensity conflict and the U.S. war against the poor, the silence of the churches and my own inadequate voice, and the immensity of the tasks that lie before us. My actions rarely keep pace with my words. The racism that low-intensity-conflict planners count on is alive within me, the individualism and mobility of our culture infect my life and emerge as obstacles to authentic community, and the hope that I with others can effectively embody a resurrection faith and seriously challenge the internal and external trappings of empire still seems distant.

However, naming the evil reduces its power over me and strengthens my resolve to confront it. I trust that the more people are willing to confront low-intensity conflict and resist the U.S. war against the poor, the greater the likelihood that we can move, sometimes awkwardly and other times more gracefully, toward a community that shares God's commitment to justice for the whole human family.

The pathway that lies before us is uncertain terrain. However, our journey will lead us to participate actively in local and global communities that express solidarity with the poor and work to overcome the causes of hunger and poverty; to order our lives in light of the unity of the body of Christ and become a leaven that raises up peace and justice within the broader human family; to embrace a provisional citizenship that prefers defense of human rights and authentic democracy over national idols and ideologies; and to become living signs of the possibilities of "living more with less" so that we can demonstrate that basic needs and spiritual health are more important and more fulfilling than mindless consumption that results in tragic poverty.

The future of the people in Central America, in our own towns and cities, and throughout the world will be shaped by how we respond to low-intensity conflict and the U.S. war against the poor. George Bush and Dan Quayle are so intimately tied to past scandals that the future isn't promising. Quayle was elected to the Senate as part of a right wing campaign to defeat senators who had worked to expose CIA and FBI abuses through the Church hearings. Robert Owen, propaganda specialist and liason between the National Security Council and the contras, worked as an aide to Senator Quayle. Quayle also had a number of meetings with John Hull whose ranch in Costa Rica has been named as a key transhipment point for illegal weapons shipments to the contras and illegal drug shipments into the United States.

Bush of course was vice president throughout the Iran-contra scandal and is a proponent of low-intensity conflict. His foreign policy aide, Donald

Gregg, was a key figure in illegal arms shipments to the contras. Gregg had frequent meetings, at times attended by Bush, with long time secret team member Felix Rodriguez. Rodriguez delivered money to the contras from the Colombian drug cartel during the time when Bush was heading up the U.S. war against drugs. Bush was also head of the CIA when many members of the "off the shelf, self-sustaining, stand alone entity" implicated in the Iran-contra affair solidified their relationships and power.

I am haunted and motivated by the words of Bishop Pedro Casaldáliga when he says that "solidarity must not tolerate too many delays. . . . You can be a Cain by killing, but you can also be a Cain by allowing others to get away with killing." Our destiny will be determined by our response to our country's war against the poor. We should add North America to the following quotation from Bishop Casaldáliga:

The route to the impending future of Latin America and the Latin American church is to be found today in Central America, and more specifically in Nicaragua. Tomorrow it will be too late. And if we fail to measure up, once again we will have been accomplices, at least by remaining silent, because we were afraid of prophecy, because we were unwilling to dirty our hands in the turbulent waters of history.[13]

Notes

1. Redefining the Enemy

1. Quoted in an article by Michael Klare, "Low Intensity Conflict: The War of the 'haves' against the 'have-nots,' " *Christianity and Crisis*, February 1, 1988, pp. 12–13.

2. Ibid., p. 12.

3. The term "third world" is problematic because it reflects the hierarchy of values and power of elite groups within the international economy and because it lumps together two-thirds of the world's people from diverse countries into a simple category. However, I decided to use this term because it is commonly used in sources that I cite throughout this book and because it is generally understood to signify countries that are not part of the highly industrialized capitalist nations (first world) or industrialized countries of the socialist bloc (second world).

4. "Developing" and "underdeveloped" are common terms used to describe poor countries in the Third World. I refer to such countries as "exploited" because this term better describes their relationship within the international economy from colonial times to the present.

5. Michael T. Klare and Peter Kornbluh, eds., *Low Intensity Warfare: Counterinsurgency, Proinsurgency, and Antiterrorism in the Eighties* (New York: Pantheon Books, 1988), p. 81.

6. Casper Weinberger, Secretary of Defense, *Annual Report to Congress Fiscal Year 1985*, (1984), p. 276. See also, Klare and Kornbluh, eds., *Low Intensity Conflict*, p. 82.

7. *Low Intensity Conflict*, Klare and Kornbluh, eds., p. 82.

8. Noam Chomsky, *Turning the Tide: U.S. Intervention in Central America and the Struggle for Peace* (Boston: South End Press, 1985), pp. 44–45.

9. Ibid., p. 47.

10. Weinberger, Secretary of Defense, *Annual Report to Congress*, p. 276.

11. Klare and Kornbluh, eds., *Low Intensity Conflict*, p. 81.

12. Ibid., p. 48

13. The Committee of Santa Fe, "A New Inter-American Policy for the Eighties" (Washington, D.C.: Council for Inter-American Security, 1980), p. 1. Cited hereafter as the Santa Fe Report.

14. Joint Low-Intensity Conflict Project, United States Army Training and Doctrine Command, "Joint Low-Intensity Conflict Project Final Report, Executive Summary," Fort Monroe, Virginia, August 1, 1986, pp. 1, 3.

15. Department of Defense, *Proceedings of the Low-Intensity Warfare Conference*, January 14–15, 1986, p. 10. See also Klare and Kornbluh, eds., *Low Intensity Warfare*, pp. 54–55.

16. The Santa Fe Report, p. ii.

17. "Report on the National Bipartisan Commission on Central America," January 1984, p. 93. This report is commonly referred to as the Kissinger Commission Report, named after its chairperson, Henry Kissinger.

18. The Santa Fe Report, p. 1.

19. Ibid.

20. Frank A. Barnett, et al., eds., *Special Operations in U.S. Strategy* (Washington, D.C.: National Defense University Press, 1984), p. 194. See also Sara Miles, "Getting On with the Ballgame," *NACLA Report* (April/May 1986), p. 19.

21. Colonel John Waghelstein, "Post Vietnam Counterinsurgency Doctrine," *Military Review* (January 1985), p. 42. *NACLA Report* (April/May 1986), p. 19.

22. Ruth Leger Sivard, *World Military and Social Expenditures*, 1986, (World Priorities Inc., Box 25140, Washington, D.C. 20007).

23. Dr. Norman Meyers, ed., *GAIA: An Atlas of Planet Management* (New York: Anchor Press/Doubleday & Company, 1984).

24. Jack Nelson-Pallmeyer, *The Politics of Compassion* (Maryknoll, N.Y.: Orbis Books, 1987), p. 99.

25. For more detail, see, for example, Jack A. Nelson, *Hunger for Justice: The Politics of Food and Faith* (Maryknoll, N.Y.: Orbis Books, 1980), and Jack Nelson-Pallmeyer, *The Politics of Compassion*.

26. Frances Moore Lappe and Joseph Collins, *World Hunger: Twelve Myths* (New York: Grove Press, 1986), p. 6.

27. OXFAM America, "Third World Debt: Payable in Hunger," *Facts for Action*, no. 16, p. 4.

28. This statistic is from a talk given by Dr. Chandra Hardy, "Global Debt/Social Turmoil," at a conference entitled "Forgive Us Our Debts" at Pacific Lutheran University, February 20, 1988.

29. *Facts for Action*, no. 16, p. 3.

30. Susan George, *A Fate Worse Than Debt*, (New York: Grove Press, 1988). See also *Facts for Action*, p. 1.

31. *Facts for Action*, pp. 3–4.

2. The "Crimes" of the Poor

1. Reagan administration ambassador to Costa Rica, Lewis A. Tambs, and Lieutenant Commander Frank Aker, "Shattering the Vietnam Sydrome: A Scenario for Success in El Salvador" (unpublished manuscript). See Michael T. Klare and Peter Kornbluh, eds., *Low Intensity Warfare: Counterinsurgency, Proinsurgency, and Antiterrorism in the Eighties* (New York: Pantheon Books, 1988), p. 112.

2. William I. Robinson and Kent Norsworthy, *David and Goliath: The U.S. War against Nicaragua* (New York: Monthly Review Press, 1987), p. 9.

3. Jeane Kirkpatrick, "Dictatorships and Double Standards," *Commentary*, November, 1979, p. 44.

4. Walter Brueggemann, *The Prophetic Imagination* (Philadelphia: Fortress Press, 1978), p. 46.

5. For a more detailed examination of liberation theology, see Jack Nelson-Pallmeyer, *The Politics of Compassion* (Maryknoll, N.Y.: Orbis Books, 1987), or Phillip Berryman, *Liberation Theology: The Essential Facts about the Revolutionary*

Movement in Latin America and Beyond (New York, Pantheon Books, 1987).

6. There are many excellent books and other resources on Nicaragua. See, for example, William I. Robinson and Kent Norsworthy, *David and Goliath*; Joseph Collins, *What Difference Could a Revolution Make?* (San Francisco: Institute for Food and Development Policy, 1986); and an Americas Watch Report (July 1985) entitled "Human Rights in Nicaragua: Reagan, Rhetoric and Reality."

7. Bishop Pedro Casaldáliga, *Prophets in Combat* (Oak Park, Ill.: Meyer Stone Books, 1986), pp. 46–47.

8. Department of Defense, *Proceedings of the Low-Intensity Warfare Conference*, January 14–15, 1986, p. 10.

3. Low-Intensity Conflict: The Strategy

1. Father Cesar Jerez, S.J., "What We Have Seen and Heard in Nicaragua," Witness for Peace On-the-Scene Reports, 1987, p. 4.

2. Bishop Pedro Casaldáliga, *Prophets in Combat* (Oak Park, Ill.: Meyer Stone Books, 1986), pp. xii–xiii.

3. "No Business Like War Business," *The Defense Monitor* 16, no. 3:1.

4. William I. Robinson and Kent Norsworthy, *David and Goliath: The U.S. War against Nicaragua* (New York: Monthly Review Press, 1987), p. 26.

5. U.S. Army, *U.S. Psychological Operations Field Manual, 33–1* (Washington, D.C.: Department of the Army, August 1979), p. H–3.

6. *The CIA's Nicaragua Manual, Psychological Operations in Guerrilla Warfare* (New York: Random House, 1985), p. 33.

7. Robinson and Norsworthy, *David and Goliath*, p. 177.

8. Klare, "Low-intensity Conflict: The War of the 'haves' against the 'have-nots,' " *Christianity and Crisis*, February 1, 1988.

9. "Affidavit of Edgar Chamorro," Case concerning Military and Paramilitary Activities in and against Nicaragua (Nicaragua v. United States of America), International Court of Justice, September 5, 1985, pp. 20–21.

10. Catholic Institute for International Relations, *Nicaragua: The Right to Survive* (Croton-on-Hudson, N.Y.: North River Press, 1987).

11. "What We Have Seen and Heard in Nicaragua," Witness for Peace on-the-Scene Reports, 1986, p. 7.

12. Robinson and Norsworthy, *David and Goliath*, pp. 56–57.

13. Witness for Peace on-the-Scene Reports, p. 5.

14. "Affidavit of Edgar Chamorro," p. 21.

15. Bob Woodward, *Veil: The Secret Wars of the CIA* (New York: Simon & Schuster, 1987), pp. 195, 173.

16. Robinson and Norsworthy, *David and Goliath*, pp. 71–72.

17. "Affidavit of Edgar Chamorro," p. 17.

18. "Contra Forces Target Civilian Medical Work in Northern Nicaragua," Executive Summary Report, U.S. Medical Task Force Investigation, January 1988.

19. Robinson and Norsworthy, *David and Goliath*, p. 36.

20. "Human Rights in Nicaragua: Reagan, Rhetoric and Reality," Americas Watch Report, July 1985, p. 1.

21. Ibid.

22. Robinson and Norsworthy, *David and Goliath*, p. 210.

23. Jack Nelson-Pallmeyer, *The Politics of Compassion* (Maryknoll, N.Y.: Orbis Books, 1987), p. 119.

24. Ibid., pp. 1–2.

25. Robinson and Norsworthy, *David and Goliath*, p. 55.

26. Americas Watch Report, July 1985, pp. 3–4.

27. Leslie Cockburn, *Out of Control* (New York: Atlantic Monthly Press, 1987).

28. Americas Watch Report, July 1985, p. 73.

29. John A. Booth, *The End and the Beginning: The Nicaraguan Revolution* (Boulder, Colo.: Westview Press, 1985), pp. 253–54.

30. "Peace Efforts Cost Costa Rica dearly," *San Francisco Bay Guardian*, August 26, 1987.

31. "Affidavit of Edgar Chamorro," p. 11.

32. Americas Watch Report, July 1985, pp. 4–5.

33. U.S. Army, *Psychological Operations Techniques and Procedures, Field Manual* 33–5 (Washington, D.C.: Department of the Army, 1966).

34. Robinson and Norsworthy, *David and Goliath*, pp. 63, 77.

35. Americas Watch Report, July 1985, p. 3.

36. Ibid., p. 233.

4. Distorted Democracy

1. The quote from Poindexter is from testimony before the Joint Select Committee, July 19, 1987. The quote from North is from an undated letter to Robert Owen. Both are found in *In Contempt of Congress: The Reagan Record on Central America*, The Institute for Policy Studies, Washington, D.C., 1987, pp. 8–9.

2. Jack A. Nelson, *Hunger for Justice: The Politics of Food and Faith* (Maryknoll, N.Y.: Orbis Books, 1980), p. 40.

3. Ibid., p. 59.

4. Frances Moore Lappe and Joseph Collins, *World Hunger: Twelve Myths* (New York: Grove Press, 1986), pp. 4–5.

5. Nelson, *Hunger for Justice*, p. 41.

6. Holly Sklar, ed., *Trilateralism: The Trilateral Commission and Elite Planning for World Management* (Boston: South End Press, 1980).

7. This quotation is taken from the written transcript of a Public Affairs Television special, with Bill Moyers, entitled *The Secret Government: The Constitution in Crisis*. The program was a production of Alvin H. Perlmutter, Inc., and Public Affairs Television, Inc., in association with WNET and WETA. Copyright 1987 by Alvin H. Perlmutter, Inc., Public Affairs Television, Inc. The written transcrpit was produced by Journal Graphics, Inc., New York, New York. Quotations from this transcript are hereafter cited as from *The Secret Government*.

8. Ibid., p. 14.

9. "Affidavit of Daniel P. Sheehan," filed on December 12, 1986, with minor revisions January 31, 1987. The affidavit is available from the Christic Institute, 1324 North Capitol Street, NW, Washington, D.C. 20002. Further quotations from this source will be referred to as "Affidavit of Daniel P. Sheehan."

10. This quotation is taken from a pamphlet produced by the Christic Institute, "Contragate, the Constitution and the 1988 Elections."

11. For specific information on the illegal weapons shipments and flow of drugs,

see Leslie Cockburn, *Out of Control* (New York: Atlantic Monthly Press, 1987).

12. Ibid.

13. This quotation is taken from an information sheet put out by the Coalition for a New Foreign Policy, 712 G Street SE, Washington, D.C. 20003.

14. Jack Nelson-Pallmeyer, *The Politics of Compassion*, (Maryknoll, N.Y.: Orbis Books, 1987), p. 119.

15. For a provocative critique of the U.S. media from the perspective of a Marxist sociologist, see Michael Parenti, Inventing Reality: The Politics of the Mass Media (New York: St. Martin's Press, 1987).

16. There are, of course, exceptions. People who want to travel to third-world nations such as Mexico, the Philippines, the countries in Central America and the Mideast with the specific purpose of exploring the causes of poverty and the impact of U.S. policies can contact the Center for Global Education, Augsburg College, 731–21st Avenue South, Minneapolis, MN 55454. The center leads approximately forty travel seminars each year to the countries listed above. Most trips are for approximately two weeks.

17. Parenti, *Inventing Reality*, p. 6.

18. Ibid., p. 27.

19. This quotation is taken from the October/November 1987 issue of *Extra*, the newsletter of FAIR (Fairness & Accuracy in Reporting), vol. 1, no. 4, p. 1.

20. "Reagan Sees to It That 'Peace Process' Won't Hinder Contra Plans," *St. Paul Pioneer Press*, January 28, 1988.

21. *The Tower Commission Report* (New York: Random House, 1987), pp. xi, xvi.

22. Ibid., p. 14.

23. Bishop Pedro Casaldáliga, *Prophets in Combat* (Oak Park, Ill.: Meyer Stone Books, 1987), pp. 24–25.

24. Ralph McGhee, "Foreign Policy by Forgery," *The Nation 11* (April 1981).

25. William I.Robinson and Kent Norsworthy, *David and Goliath: The U.S. War against Nicaragua* (New York: Monthly Review Press, 1987), pp. 36–37.

26. *Miami Herald*, July 19, 1987.

27. See Cockburn, *Out of Control*, p. 35, and "Affidavit of Daniel P. Sheehan," p. 16.

28. Parenti, *Inventing Reality*, pp. 6–7.

29. *The Secret Government*, p. 5.

30. Ibid., p. 13.

31. James Bamford, *The Puzzle Palace* (New York: Penguin Books, 1983), p. 477.

32. "Affidavit of Daniel P. Sheehan," p. 5.

33. *The Secret Government*, p. 18.

34. Information on Salvadoran death squads operating in the United States can be found in *NACLA Report*, vol. 21, no. 3.

35. Robert Boyden Lamb, "Ruthless Leaders," *Success* magazine, June 1988, p. 42.

36. *Bill Moyers' Journal:Campaign Report #3* (1983), p. 7. This is a transcrpit of a document aired on WNET, channel 13, by the Educational Broadcasting Corporation.

5. Faith and Empire

1. Walter Brueggemann, *The Creative Imagination* (Philadelphia: Fortress Press, 1978), pp. 20–21.

2. Ibid., p. 11.

3. Ibid., pp. 15–17.

4. Ibid., p. 17.

5. Paul D. Hanson, *The People Called: The Growth of Community in the Bible* (New York: Harper & Row, 1986), pp. 2–3.

6. For a more complete discussion of this issue, see Nelson-Pallmeyer, *The Politics of Compassion* (Maryknoll, N.Y.: Orbis Books, 1987), chap. 5.

7. Ulrich Duchrow, *Global Economy: A Confessional Issue for the Churches* (Geneva: World Council of Churches Publications, 1987), pp. 92–93.

8. Ibid.; this quotation is found before the table of contents.

9. Robert McAfee Brown, *Saying Yes and Saying No* (Philadelphia: Westminister Press, 1986), pp. 16–17.

10. *Lutheran Book of Worship* (Minneapolis and Philadelphia: Augsburg Publishing House and Board of Publication of the Lutheran Church in America, 1978), p. 77.

11. Duchrow, *Global Economy*, pp. 47–48.

12. Kavanaugh, *Following Christ in a Consumer Culture*, (Maryknoll, N.Y.: Orbis Books, 1981) pp. 42–43.

13. Bishop Pedro Casaldáliga, *Prophets in Combat*, (Oak Park, Ill.: Meyer Stone Books, 1987), pp. 11, 14.

Index